Future-Ready Data Foundation with MongoDB

Principles for designing scalable and AI-ready data architectures

Sarah Evans

<packt>

Future-Ready Data Foundation with MongoDB

Portfolio Director: Sunith Shetty
Relationship Lead: Sathya Mohan
Project Manager: Sathya Mohan
Content Engineer: Siddhant Jain
Technical Editor: Shweta Amale
Copy Editor: Siddhant Jain
Proofreader: Siddhant Jain
Production Designer: Deepak Chavan
Growth Lead: Varun Nair

First published: June 2026

Production reference: 1060726

Published by Packt Publishing Ltd.
Grosvenor House
11 St Paul's Square
Birmingham
B3 1RB, UK.

ISBN 978-1-80760-717-3
www.packtpub.com

Foreword

We are at an unusual moment. The tools for building AI-powered systems have never been more accessible, and the pressure to deploy them has never been higher. But accessibility and readiness are different things, and the gap between them is where most AI initiatives run into trouble. That gap is not a model problem, not a talent problem, and not a budget problem, it's almost always a data infrastructure problem.

This book is about getting that foundation right. It addresses the data infrastructure challenges that cause AI initiatives to stall in production and offers practical guidance grounded in how these systems behave at scale. The two scenarios woven throughout the chapters, an insurance carrier building a claims processing agent and a logistics company deploying predictive maintenance across a large fleet, reflect the kind of complexity that engineers and technology leaders encounter in real projects. They represent the kinds of challenges where the right architectural decisions make a meaningful difference.

The guidance here, on unified data models, retrieval strategies, scalability patterns, and governance, draws from what we have seen work in production environments where the stakes are real. MongoDB has spent years working alongside organizations navigating exactly these challenges, and this book reflects that experience.

Whether you are modernizing your organization's data platform or making the architectural decisions that will determine whether your AI investments pay off, we hope this book gives you a clearer picture of the landscape and the confidence to move forward.

The MongoDB University Team

Contributors

About the author

Sarah Evans is a Senior Curriculum Engineer at MongoDB, where she designs and develops technical learning experiences for MongoDB University. With a background that bridges curriculum design and hands-on technical expertise, she specializes in translating complex database and data modeling concepts into clear, accessible content for developers and technology professionals. Sarah is passionate about making technical education practical and engaging, drawing on her experience developing curricula that empowers learners to apply knowledge in real-world scenarios. Since joining MongoDB in 2021, she has contributed to a wide range of educational initiatives spanning data modeling, database architecture, and developer enablement. Sarah is also deeply interested in AI-driven development and building AI-powered products, and she brings that enthusiasm to her work helping learners navigate the intersection of modern databases and intelligent application design.

About the reviewers

Rita Rodrigues is a Director of Curriculum at MongoDB, where she leads customer technical curriculum development. She began her career in software engineering and has worked as a developer, scrum master, architect, and data engineer before focusing her career on helping developers grow through strong technical education. Over the course of her career, she has led cross-functional teams, including developers, solution architects, content strategists, and developer advocates, all with a focus on building meaningful learning experiences and enabling developer communities. Originally from Lisbon and now based in Dublin, Rita brings both deep technical experience and an international perspective to her work. She holds a master's degree in computer science and is passionate about making technical knowledge easier to develop, share, and apply.

Emily Pope is a Senior Manager, Technical Curriculum at MongoDB. She loves learning and is passionate about making it easy for others to learn how and when to use deeply technical products. Her team is responsible for creating skill badges focused on Search, Vector Search, and AI, in addition to the core database. Beyond skill badges, the team develops AI tools to support the creation of technically sound learning content used by teams across MongoDB. Before joining MongoDB, she created learning experiences on databases, computer science, full-stack development, and even clinical trial design and analysis. Emily holds an Ed.M. in International Education Policy from Harvard Graduate School of Education and began her career as an English teacher in Türkiye with the Fulbright Program.

Manuel Fontan is a Staff Technologist on MongoDB's Curriculum team, where he focuses on AI-assisted curriculum development and GenAI education. He has contributed to MongoDB University's AI and Search training portfolio across topics including vector search, RAG, AI agents, memory, and Voyage AI integrations. He has also led the development of Curriculum AI tools to improve the speed, consistency, and quality of content creation and maintenance. Previously, Manuel was a Senior Technical Services Engineer on MongoDB's Core team. Between his two tenures at MongoDB, he worked for a little over two years as a Database Reliability Engineer at Slack and later at Cognite before rejoining the company. With more than 15 years of experience in software development and distributed systems, Manuel is naturally curious and holds an MSc in Telecommunications Engineering from the University of Vigo, Spain, and an MSc in Free and Open Source Software from Rey Juan Carlos University, Spain.

Parker Faucher is a Senior Curriculum Engineer on the MongoDB University team, where he designs and develops technical learning content for developers and data professionals. Based in Phoenix, Arizona, Parker specializes in building skills-based learning experiences across topics such as vector search, AI applications, and MongoDB performance, helping learners move from concept to hands-on practice. With a strong focus on quality and efficiency, Parker also leads efforts to integrate AI tools into the curriculum development workflow, streamlining reviews, accelerating iteration cycles, and freeing up more time for the work that matters most.

MongoDB Skill Badges

After reading this book, you can validate and showcase your knowledge with official **MongoDB Skill Badges**, which are free, focused credentials that you can earn in just 60 to 90 minutes.

Elevate your AI skillset with badges such as:

Table of Contents

Preface

Most AI initiatives don't fail because of the models; they fail because of the underlying data infrastructure.

That is the central idea this book explores. Organizations are investing heavily in large language models, retrieval pipelines, and AI agents, and too many of them are watching those investments stall in production, not because the AI is inadequate, but because its foundation wasn't built for what AI requires.

The problem is rarely visible in testing. It emerges in production. Data fragmented across disconnected systems starts slowing down retrieval. Governance gaps surface sensitive records that were never meant to reach an AI pipeline. Vector search infrastructure that handled a few thousand documents buckles under the weight of a million. By then, the damage is already done, to organizational trust and customer trust alike.

This book is about building a foundation that holds up when it counts. It focuses on the three core requirements that any AI-ready data infrastructure must meet:

- The ability to manage diverse data types in a single system
- Intelligent retrieval that surfaces the right information at the right time
- Processing patterns that keep AI pipelines responsive and trustworthy at scale

Chapter by chapter, you'll see how MongoDB is designed to meet all three without the complexity of stitching together multiple specialized tools.

Throughout the book, two scenarios serve as recurring anchors: a regional insurance carrier building an AI-powered claims processing agent and a national logistics company deploying a predictive maintenance system across a fleet of thousands of trucks. These are hypothetical use cases, but they reflect patterns we see across industries, from healthcare and financial services to manufacturing and legal services.

By the end of this book, you will have a clear framework for evaluating your current data infrastructure, understanding where the gaps are, and making informed decisions about the platform choices that will determine whether your AI initiatives succeed or stall.

Who this book is for

This book is for technology and business leaders responsible for modernizing data platforms and preparing their organizations for AI-driven workloads, including CTOs, CIOs, CDOs, heads of architecture, and digital transformation leaders. Deep technical expertise is not required, but readers should have experience with enterprise technology decision-making and familiarity with cloud and data strategy concepts.

What this book covers

Chapter 1, Building a Unified Data Foundation for Sustainable AI Modernization, introduces the data infrastructure challenges that cause AI initiatives to stall and establishes the three core requirements every AI-ready platform must meet: managing diverse data types, enabling intelligent retrieval, and supporting timely processing.

Chapter 2, Selecting the Right Retrieval Strategy for AI Workloads, covers why keyword-based search fails in AI applications and how vector and hybrid retrieval approaches deliver more accurate, contextually relevant results in production.

Chapter 3, How MongoDB's Architecture Supports Modern AI, shows how MongoDB's flexible document model and native vector search, powered by Voyage AI, consolidate the data and retrieval capabilities that AI applications need into a single platform.

Chapter 4, How Replication, Sharding, and Workload Isolation Keep AI Systems Running, covers how MongoDB's replication, automatic failover, sharding, and dedicated Search Nodes keep AI systems available and scalable as workloads grow.

Chapter 5, Eliminating the Hidden Cost of AI Infrastructure with MongoDB, explains why vector indexes are memory-intensive and walks through the three primary options for addressing performance degradation in production: dedicated Search Nodes, quantization, and index optimization with views.

Chapter 6, Governance and Compliance for AI-Ready Organizations, explains why governance requirements must be established before AI systems go into production and walks through MongoDB's built-in capabilities for access control, auditing, permissions management, and multi-tenant data isolation.

As AI becomes a core part of business operations, the question is not whether organizations will adopt AI, but whether their data infrastructure is prepared to support it in production. The organizations that succeed will be those that can unify their data, retrieve relevant information, and operate at scale without introducing unnecessary complexity. This book explores how MongoDB addresses these requirements and covers key principles for evaluating and modernizing your AI infrastructure.

AI systems are only as effective as the infrastructure that delivers the data they depend on. This book is about building that foundation.

To get the most out of this book

You should have a general understanding of modern data platforms, cloud computing, and enterprise technology concepts. Although not required, familiarity with AI terminology, data management, enterprise architecture, and MongoDB can help you get more value from the examples and discussions throughout the book.

Download the color images

Your purchase includes a color, DRM-free PDF copy of this book, ideal for viewing color images, screenshots, and diagrams. Refer to *Free benefits with your book section* at the end of the *Preface* to unlock your PDF copy.

Conventions used

There are a number of text conventions used throughout this book.

`CodeInText`: Indicates code words in text, database table names, folder names, filenames, file extensions, pathnames, dummy URLs, user input, and Twitter handles. For example: "MongoDB supports permissions at the database level, the collection level, or scoped to specific actions such as `find`, `insert`, and `aggregate`."

A block of code is set as follows:

```
{
  "_id": "claim-00482",
  "policy_no": "AUTO-9842331",
  "status": "under_review",
  "claimant": {
    "id": "C102938",
    "name": "Marie Tremblay",
    "prior_claims": 1
  },
```

Bold: Indicates a new term, an important word, or words that you see on the screen. For instance, "At present, two AI architectures dominate enterprise adoption: **retrieval-augmented generation** (RAG) systems and **AI agents.**"

> Warnings or important notes appear like this.

> Tips and tricks appear like this.

Get in touch

Feedback from our readers is always welcome.

General feedback: If you have questions about any aspect of this book or have any general feedback, please email us at `customercare@packt.com` and mention the book's title in the subject of your message.

Errata: Although we have taken every care to ensure the accuracy of our content, mistakes do happen. If you have found a mistake in this book, we would be grateful if you reported this to us. Please visit http://www.packt.com/submit-errata, click **Submit Errata**, and fill in the form.

Piracy: If you come across any illegal copies of our works in any form on the internet, we would be grateful if you would provide us with the location address or website name. Please contact us at `copyright@packt.com` with a link to the material.

If you are interested in becoming an author: If there is a topic that you have expertise in and you are interested in either writing or contributing to a book, please visit `http://authors.packt.com`

Free benefits with your book

This book includes free benefits designed to support your learning and help you apply what you learn effectively. Activate them now for instant access (see the *How to unlock* section for instructions).

Here's a quick overview of what you can instantly unlock with your purchase:

Complete Code Bundle

Download the full source code for this book's examples and projects.

DRM-Free PDF Version

Download DRM-free PDF and ePub copies of this book.

7-Day Packt Library Access

Get 7-day unlimited access to 8,000+ books and videos. No credit card required.

Available for first-time Packt+ trial users only.

Next-Gen Reader Access

Read this book on Packt Reader with progress sync, dark mode and note-taking.

How to unlock

Scan the QR code (or go to packtpub.com/unlock). Search for this book by name, confirm the edition, and then follow the steps on the page.

UNLOCK NOW

Note: Have your invoice handy. Purchases made directly from the Packt website don't require an invoice.

Share your thoughts

Once you've read *Future-Ready Data Foundation with MongoDB*, we'd love to hear your thoughts! Scan the QR code below to go straight to the Amazon review page for this book and share your feedback.

https://packt.link/r/1807607178

Your review is important to us and the tech community and will help us make sure we're delivering excellent quality content.

1

Building a Unified Data Foundation for Sustainable AI Modernization

Why do AI initiatives stall? Is it a shortage of talent? A lack of access to capable models? Or insufficient investment in cloud infrastructure? These are the usual suspects, but the real answer almost always traces back to infrastructure gaps that exist because of choices made years earlier, often long before anyone was thinking seriously about AI at scale. Legacy systems were built to store and retrieve data for humans, not to feed intelligent agents operating at speed. Data was siloed by department and not designed for cross-system reasoning. Governance frameworks were built around compliance checklists, not the dynamic, high-velocity access patterns that AI demands. These gaps are rarely visible until a promising initiative reaches production, and then they become impossible to ignore. Understanding them is the first step toward building a foundation that is truly ready for what AI requires.

In this chapter, you will:

- Identify the most common challenges organizations face when building AI initiatives
- Understand the architecture of **retrieval-augmented generation** (**RAG**) systems
- Explore the core capabilities of AI agents
- Recognize the shared data requirements of these systems, including diverse data types, real-time processing, and intelligent retrieval

Why many AI initiatives stall

Before we can define what a strong data foundation looks like, it's worth understanding why so many AI initiatives fail to get off the ground in the first place.

Take a regional insurance carrier that wants to modernize claims processing by deploying an AI agent. The system is designed to accept a claim, gather all relevant information such as policies, damaged photos, and medical records, and generate a settlement recommendation in minutes instead of days. The organization has access to modern AI models, experienced architects, and the right search and vector capabilities. In testing, the system performed flawlessly but in production, something very different happened.

The initiative unraveled across three fronts. First, policy records, claim histories, and damaged photos were spread across separate systems, forcing the agent to piece results together manually, leading to worse recommendations and eroded trust. Second, the retrieval system surfaced unstructured notes containing sensitive health information that had never been access-controlled, triggering a months-long governance overhaul. Third, vector search infrastructure that handled testing buckled under real workload, stretching settlement times from just a few minutes to fifteen or more.

Similar stories repeat across industries. This is a common pattern seen across teams trying to launch AI initiatives. But the problem isn't with the talent, the models, or the cloud infrastructure. It's the data infrastructure underneath. Teams are often relying on architectural decisions and systems that were built years earlier to solve problems that had nothing to do with AI at scale. Understanding how these gaps create challenges is the first step toward building a data foundation that is ready for what comes next.

The current AI landscape

Understanding the problem is only half the battle. To design a data foundation that holds up in production, we need to know what we're building it for. At present, two AI architectures dominate enterprise adoption: **RAG** systems and **AI agents**. They represent the most widely deployed patterns for putting AI to work on real business problems, and they place very specific requirements on the data infrastructure beneath them. Before we can define what a unified data foundation should look like, we need to understand how these systems work and what they're designed to overcome.

How RAG systems retrieve and ground responses

When you interact with a chatbot, such as Claude or ChatGPT, you are interacting with a **large language model (LLM)**, a system trained on vast amounts of public data to understand and generate human-like language. LLMs are powerful, but they have a significant limitation: they don't have access to your company's proprietary data, and they don't automatically learn about new information. Ask one about a specific policy and it may respond with a confident-sounding guess that is simply wrong, a phenomenon known as **hallucination**.

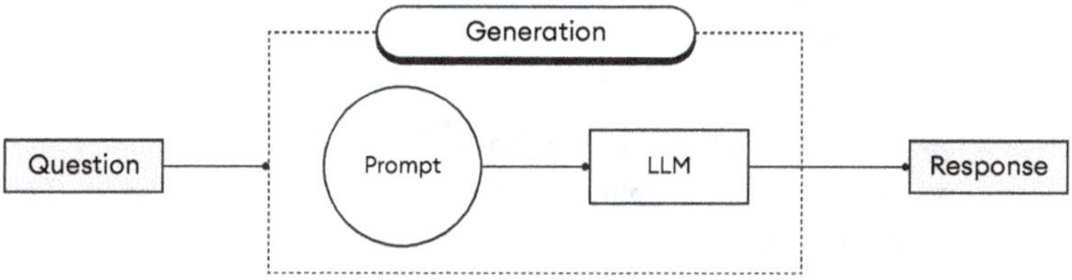

Figure 1.1 – How a chatbot like Claude generates a response

RAG solves this by first searching your own data for relevant context, then passing that context to the model alongside the original question so the response is grounded in accurate, current information. The quality of that retrieval step is everything.

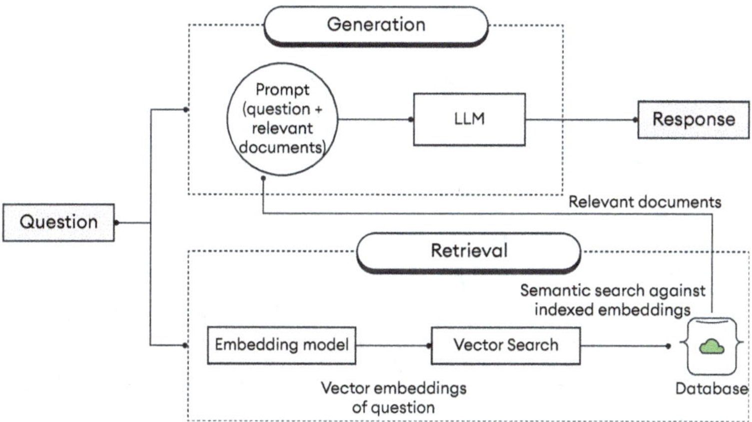

Figure 1.2 – How RAG systems retrieve relevant data as context to an LLM

RAG systems depend on your data to produce accurate answers, but that only works when the data is prepared and ingested in a way that makes it easy to retrieve the most relevant information. To understand the data and infrastructure this requires, let's consider how this process works.

The following steps walk through how a RAG system works end to end:

1. **Identify your data sources:** Company knowledge can live in many places, such as databases, documents, emails, chat histories, customer interactions, and more. The first step is knowing where your relevant data lives.
2. **Prepare and ingest your data:** Once gathered and normalized, your data needs to be converted into vector embeddings. Embeddings capture semantic meaning, so phrases such as "blocked credit card" and "fraud hold" are recognized as related even though they use different words. This requires choosing an embedding model, generating and storing embeddings, and keeping them synchronized as your data changes.

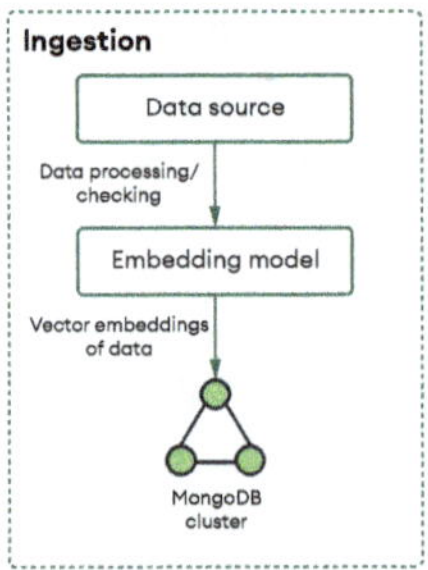

Figure 1.3 – A diagram illustrating the ingestion stage of a RAG system

> **Note**
>
> Vector embeddings are numerical representations that capture meaning. Modern databases such as MongoDB Atlas store these embeddings as lists of numbers, where each number encodes a specific aspect of the data's meaning.

3. **Retrieve the right data:** This stage involves querying a knowledge base (such as a vector database) with the user's input to find and return the most relevant documents or passages. To do this really well, you need both semantic and lexical search capabilities, as required by your use case. We'll cover these approaches in depth in *Chapter 2, Selecting the Right Retrieval Strategy for AI Workloads.*

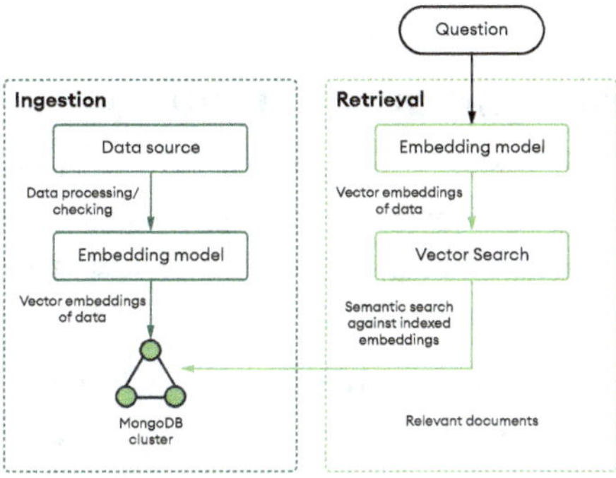

Figure 1.4 – A diagram illustrating the ingestion and retrieval stages of a RAG system

4. **Prompt the LLM:** The retrieved documents are passed to the model alongside the original question and any additional instructions. The model reads that context and generates its response. The quality of the final answer depends entirely on whether the right documents were retrieved and whether they contain accurate, current information.

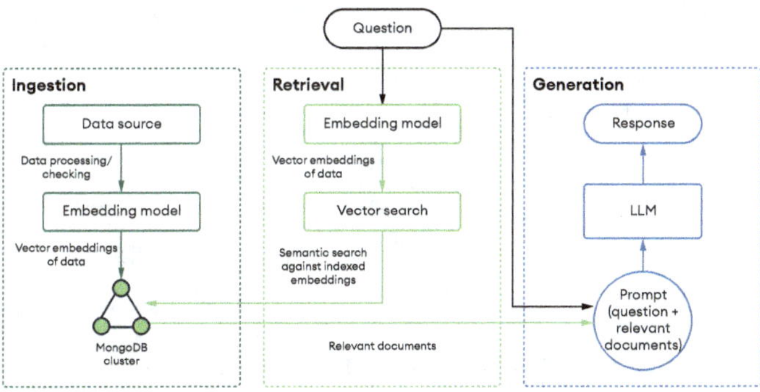

Figure 1.5 – A diagram illustrating the ingestion, retrieval, and generation stages of a RAG system

Each stage of this process, from data preparation to retrieval to response generation, has its own requirements, and those stages have to work together smoothly for the system to deliver accurate, trustworthy answers. That coordination is easy to achieve when your data infrastructure is clean and consolidated but it becomes increasingly difficult as system sprawl grows. The more your data is scattered across disconnected systems, the more places there are for something to break down.

AI agents and autonomous workflows

RAG systems are powerful for retrieval and question answering. But there is a large class of business problems that require systems that can perceive their environment, reason through complex tasks, and take action autonomously. These systems are known as AI agents.

An AI agent is an autonomous system that can accomplish multi-step tasks without manual intervention at each step. By combining an LLM with planning capabilities, tools, and memory, an AI agent can break down complex goals into subtasks, execute actions, and adapt based on the results.

How AI agents work

An AI agent is a system with several interconnected capabilities. First, it **perceives.** An agent receives input, usually a user request or a triggering event, such as a customer submitting an insurance claim.

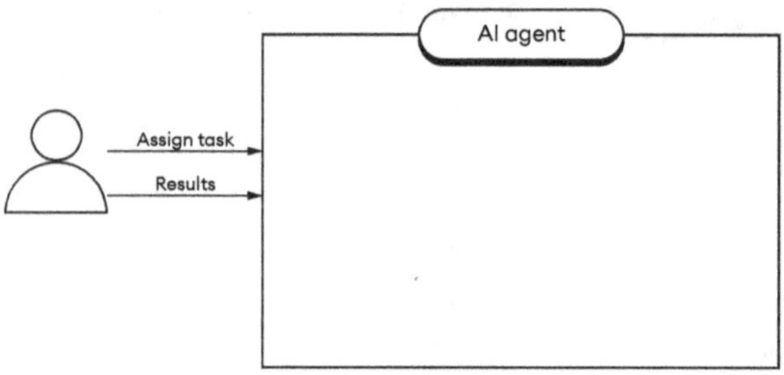

Figure 1.6 – An AI agent perceiving an assigned task

Second, it **reasons.** The agent uses an LLM to understand what the user is asking for and what actions are needed to fulfill that request. It breaks the goal into steps. "To process this claim, I need to: retrieve the policy, assess the damage description, check for any red flags, calculate a preliminary settlement, and draft a recommendation." The agent does not just answer questions about what it should do, it figures out the sequence of actions.

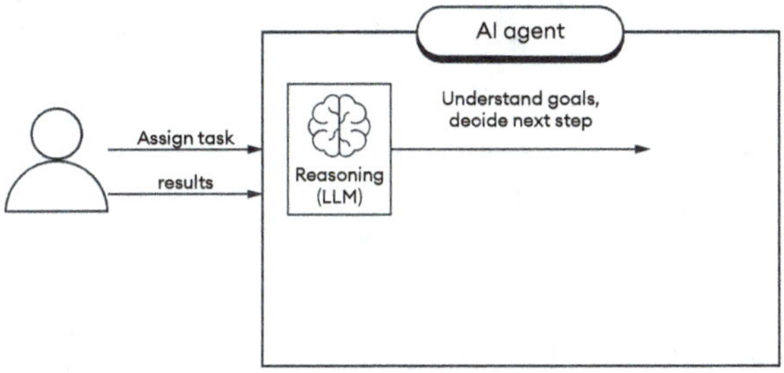

Figure 1.7 – An AI agent reasoning to understand goals and decide the next step

Third, it **acts**. Unlike a passive chatbot, an agent has access to tools that let it interact with external systems. For example, in insurance claims processing, an agent might retrieve the policy from the claims system, pull damage assessments from a document store, check compliance rules in a governance system, calculate settlement amounts, and send the recommendation to the workflow queue.

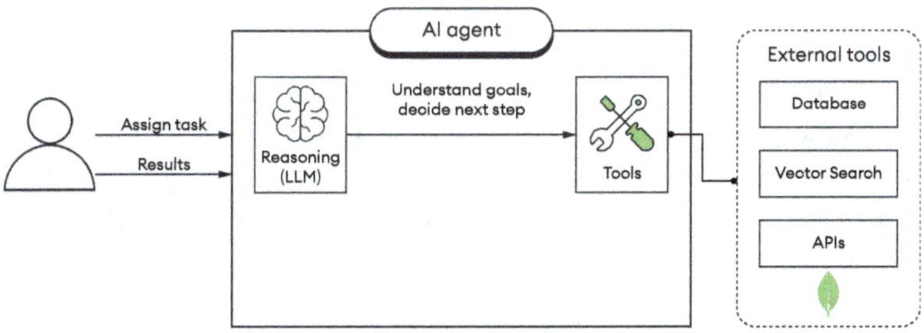

Figure 1.8 – An AI agent acting with tools to accomplish its goal(s)

Fourth, it **remembers**. An agent stores information about past interactions and uses that memory to make better decisions. If an agent has processed claims from a specific customer before, it can recall that history. Or, if it has encountered similar claims and knows what worked, it can apply that learning. Memory transforms a stateless chatbot into a system that learns and improves over time.

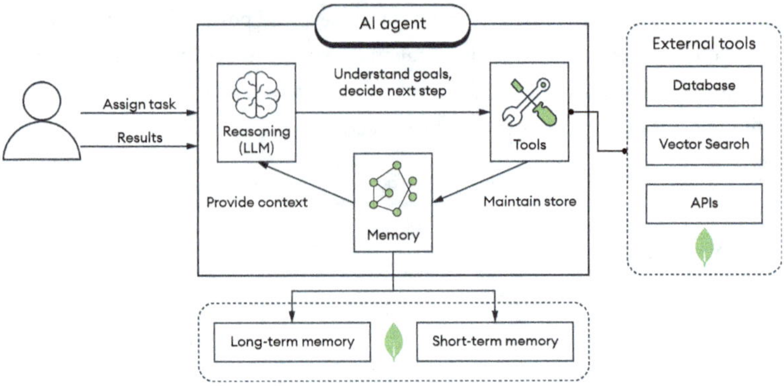

Figure 1.9 – An AI agent using memory to maintain state and provide additional context

An AI agent doing all of this simultaneously needs to handle multiple data sources, perform sophisticated retrieval, and act on fresh data in real time. When each of those steps queries a different system, the workflow becomes slow and fragile. This is why a solid data infrastructure behind an AI agent is essential for success.

Data infrastructure requirements for modern AI systems

At this point, you understand the basics of how RAG systems and AI agents work, and why they can stall. Now we need to be specific about what your data infrastructure has to do in order for your AI initiatives to succeed. There are three core requirements for your data infrastructure. The following sections examine each of these requirements and explain why they are essential for building reliable, production-ready AI systems.

Managing diverse data types efficiently and consistently

Modern AI applications work with data that comes in many forms including:

- Structured data such as customer records, policies, and transaction history
- Unstructured data like documents, emails, notes, and support tickets
- Images, videos, and audio.
- Vector embeddings that capture semantic meaning.
- Relational data, hierarchical data, and graph-based relationships

Organizations often store these data types in separate systems, but AI applications do not work in silos, they need to work with all of these data types at once. A unified data infrastructure stores all of these data types in one logical place so that when an agent needs the complete picture of a claim, it queries one system rather than five. And because all data is managed through that single system, consistency is far easier to maintain and enforce.

Enabling intelligent retrieval that goes beyond simple keyword search

Retrieval is the linchpin of both RAG and AI agents. The data your system surfaces is the data it reasons from, which means gaps or inaccuracies in retrieval translate directly into incorrect answers, faulty recommendations, misunderstood tasks, and poor business outcomes. Intelligent retrieval requires several capabilities working together: lexical search, vector search, hybrid search, and intelligent reranking. We'll cover how these approaches work in greater depth in the next chapter. A unified platform that can combine them lets your RAG pipeline or AI agent execute all of these approaches in a single query without coordinating across multiple systems. Latency stays low and performance scales because everything is local to one system.

Supporting real-time processing so AI systems can react to new information

The third requirement is support for event-driven processing when the use case genuinely demands it. For some workflows, event-driven infrastructure is essential. For example, when a suspicious transaction occurs, a fraud detection agent may need to act on that signal immediately, not hours later when a scheduled process finally delivers the necessary data. An AI system that flags a suspicious transaction in the moment and triggers an immediate downstream response can prevent damage, while one working from stale data can only document it after the fact. That said, AI systems can be on-demand, asynchronous, or scheduled depending on the use case.

These three requirements work together but how much weight you give each one depends on the AI initiative you are pursuing. A RAG system, for example, places a premium on intelligent retrieval and data quality, but may not require real-time processing at all. An AI agent monitoring live transactions, on the other hand, may demand all three in equal measure. Understanding your specific use case is the first step to knowing where to invest because building for the wrong requirements is just as costly as ignoring them altogether.

While there is no single mandatory architecture, platforms that address all three cohesively tend to produce RAG systems that perform at scale, agents that are reliable and well-suited to their use case, and infrastructure that can evolve without constant rework underneath it.

Assessing platform readiness for AI

Before committing to a data platform for your AI initiatives, it's worth considering what you are actually trying to deliver and whether your current infrastructure can get you there.

- **Data sources:** How many systems currently hold the data your AI depends on, and what does that fragmentation cost in complexity, reliability, and speed? Each system represents an integration to maintain, a potential point of failure, and a rebuilding cost every time your needs evolve. Fragmented data infrastructure can create technical debt and limits what your AI can do and how quickly you can scale.
- **Intelligent retrieval:** How effectively does your platform retrieve the right information at the right time? How many vendors are currently involved in your retrieval pipeline, and what does that complexity cost you when something goes wrong?
- **Timely and event-driven processing:** Which of your AI use cases require immediate action, and which can tolerate delay? For use cases that do require real-time processing, when something changes in your data, how quickly can your systems act on it? How many systems need to coordinate to deliver a timely response, and what happens to your customer experience when that coordination breaks down?

Asking these questions to understand where your infrastructure aligns with your goals for AI systems and where it doesn't will create the clarity needed to make intentional decisions, avoid costly rebuilds down the line, and build AI systems that scale with your business.

Summary

The insurance carrier in our opening example had capable models and experienced architects. What they lacked was a data foundation that met these three requirements: manage diverse data types, enable intelligent retrieval, and support timely and event-driven processing. And that is precisely why their initiative stalled, and why so many others do too. The limiting factor is rarely the AI itself, but the infrastructure beneath it.

In the chapters ahead, we will explore how MongoDB directly addresses each of these requirements and what that means for your organization's ability to build, scale, and securely operate AI applications at the level your business demands.

AI Data Strategy with MongoDB

Understand how MongoDB supports AI data strategies, simplifies AI infrastructure, and accelerates secure AI application development.

`https://mdb.link/badge-ai-data-strategy-press`

RAG with MongoDB

Build RAG applications, integrate vector search, optimize retrieval workflows, and enhance LLM-powered applications.

`https://mdb.link/badge-rag-press`

AI Agents with MongoDB

Build and deploy AI agents, orchestrate AI workflows, integrate AI models, and manage real-time application data.

`https://mdb.link/badge-ai-agents-press`

2

Selecting the Right Retrieval Strategy for AI Workloads

In the previous chapter, we introduced the two architectural patterns at the heart of most enterprise AI initiatives today: **retrieval-augmented generation** (**RAG**) and AI agents. You learned that both depend heavily on intelligent retrieval, or the ability to find and surface the right information at the right moment. This chapter takes a closer look at how intelligent retrieval actually works, walking through three approaches: lexical search, vector search, and hybrid retrieval.

Lexical search matches queries to documents based on exact or closely matching words, making it fast and reliable for precise terms. This approach was the foundation of enterprise search for decades.

Vector search adds something new to this picture by representing data as embeddings in a multidimensional space. This allows for matching by meaning rather than exact wording, so that your AI application can understand the way people naturally describe their problems.

Hybrid retrieval brings both approaches together by combining their results.

Understanding each of these approaches, and when to use them, will equip you to make informed architectural decisions that have a significant impact on the quality, relevance, and reliability of the responses your AI produces.

In this chapter, we will cover the following topics:

- How retrieval quality shapes AI reliability and user trust
- Where lexical and vector search each work well, and where they fall short
- How hybrid retrieval works, and when it makes sense for your organization to use it

Why search quality determines AI reliability

Imagine you're the head of customer experience at a mid-sized e-commerce company. Your team has just deployed an AI-powered customer service assistant built on RAG architecture. While the early results were promising, complaints have started trickling in.

A customer asks the chatbot: "*My package hasn't shown up and I'm really frustrated, what are my options?*" The assistant responds with a list of shipping partners and delivery timeframes. However, what the customer is actually looking for is information about refunds, reshipments, and how to file a claim. As a result, they leave even more frustrated than before.

What went wrong? In this case, it wasn't the AI model that failed; it was the search layer underneath.

The search layer underneath

Before an AI system, such as a RAG application, can generate a response, it has to find the right information to base that response on. The component responsible for that search is called the retrieval layer. We can think of it as a research assistant who, before answering your question, scans through a vast library of documents to find the most relevant ones. The quality of that assistant's answer depends entirely on whether they found the right material.

For decades, the dominant method for pulling those files has been **full-text search**, also called **lexical search**. When a user submits a query, the system scans its index for documents containing matching words, then ranks results based on factors such as term frequency and rarity. This approach still powers tools such as Elasticsearch and many enterprise search products, and is fast and effective when users know exactly what words to use.

Problems appear with lexical search when human language contains variation and nuance. Our frustrated customer didn't type "refund" or "missing package claim." They described their situation in plain, emotional language. During the retrieval stage, the RAG system used a lexical search engine, scanning for keyword matches, and found the word "*options*" appearing frequently in shipping documents and surfaced those instead. It had no way of understanding that "*hasn't shown up*" means "*lost in transit.*"

This is the core limitation of lexical search: **it matches words, not meaning.** In enterprise environments, this gap is everywhere. A sales rep searching for "discount approval process" might never find a document titled "Pricing Exception Guidelines" even when it contains exactly what they need. This failure mode is called retrieval failure. The LLM at the center of your AI product may be capable of reasoning. However, if it wasn't originally trained on your proprietary data, it can only work with what the retrieval layer hands it. Poor retrieval means poor answers.

When an AI application gives a customer a plausible-sounding but incorrect answer, the failure is rarely the language model. It's almost always the search layer underneath.

The good news is that this problem is solvable, with the evolution from lexical to semantic search closing this gap.

How modern search has changed and why it matters

In the last section, we left our frustrated customer without a resolution. Their experience points to a question that researchers and engineers spent years trying to answer: what if a search system could understand what someone *means*, not just what they *type*?

The answer arrived through a change in how machines represent language. That change expanded what is possible in search and, by extension, in AI systems that rely on retrieval.

Teaching machines to understand meaning

To understand the shift, it helps to think about how meaning actually works. When you read the phrase "my package hasn't shown up," you instantly understand it as a problem of non-delivery. You make that connection not because you've memorized a list of synonyms, but because years of experience have taught you that these words, in this context, describe a specific kind of situation.

For a long time, machines couldn't do this. Words were just strings of characters that were either identical or different, present or absent. Even where similarity search was possible, there was no understanding of the relationship between ideas.

Vector embeddings changed this by enabling semantic similarity, or the ability to find related concepts even when exact words aren't used.

Embeddings are numerical representations of data, such as words, sentences, or even images that capture their meaning in a way that allows for semantic understanding. We can think of vector embeddings as coordinates on a map, where similar ideas cluster together. So, "my package hasn't shown up" might be clustered near "missing delivery," "order never arrived," and "shipment not received" even though none of those phrases share a single word.

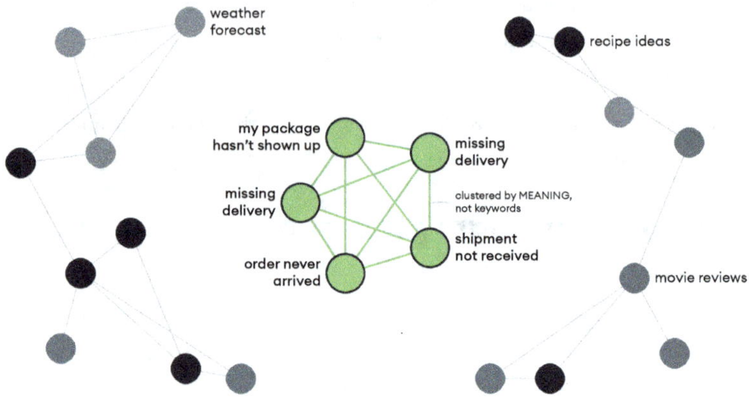

Figure 2.1 – Embeddings clustered by meaning in a high-dimensional space

These coordinates exist in high-dimensional space. A typical embedding might contain 1,024 dimensions or numbers, where each number represents a learned feature of meaning that the model discovered during training. While we cannot visualize 1,024 dimensions, the principle is the same as our map analogy, where the closer two points are, the more similar their meanings.

Before search time, an embedding model is used to convert data in your knowledge base into a vector and store those vectors in the database alongside the original content. Think of this as pre-plotting every document on the map before anyone arrives to ask a question. Then, when a user submits a query, that query is converted into a vector using the same embedding model, placing it as a coordinate on the same map, and the system finds the data whose coordinates sit closest to it.

> **Note**
>
> Embedding models convert text into numbers that capture meaning, making it possible to compare and search content by intent rather than exact words. Unlike LLMs, embedding models don't read, reason, or generate responses. They simply encode meaning into a format that can be compared and searched. An LLM is the expert that drafts the answer; an embedding model is the system that determines what that expert should be looking at.

To measure that closeness, we use similarity metrics. Cosine similarity, which calculates the angle between two vectors, is the most common choice for text embeddings. A smaller angle means that concepts are more closely related. Other techniques include dot product similarity and Euclidean distance, each with slightly different characteristics, but all serving the same purpose: quantifying how semantically similar two pieces of content are.

This is the foundation of **vector search**, also called **semantic search**, where vector closeness corresponds to semantic similarity. Instead of scanning for keyword matches, the system converts the query into vectors, then finds the content within the database whose vector is closest to the query's vector. It's searching by meaning rather than by words.

Back to the filing cabinet

Think again of the research assistant in the library. Lexical search gave that assistant an index of every word in every document. The assistant could find any document containing the word "refund" quickly but would miss content listed under different terminology.

Vector search gives the assistant something closer to a sense of what each document is about. When our customer asks, "*what are my options,*" the assistant no longer depends on that exact phrasing. It recognizes the underlying intent, a person seeking remedies for a fulfillment problem, and surfaces the claims process document, the reshipment policy, and the refund FAQ. The words differ in these documents, but the meaning aligns.

For our ecommerce customer service assistant, adopting vector search significantly changes results because product descriptions, support articles, and policy documents become discoverable through the natural language that customers use. This narrows the gap between how the organization writes and how customers speak.

How semantic search powers trustworthy AI responses

Retrieval quality is both a search and trust problem. Every time an internal knowledge assistant cites an outdated policy, it creates friction, confusion, or even a compliance risk.

Vector search addresses this because it retrieves by meaning rather than by keyword. This makes it more resilient to the language variability that breaks lexical systems. In a RAG system, similar to our example, that resilience compounds. Better retrieval means more accurate grounding. More accurate grounding means more trustworthy responses. More trustworthy responses mean a system your customers, employees, and leadership can actually rely on.

We've focused on RAG systems in this example, but vector search impacts AI agents too. An agent, by contrast, retrieves context to make decisions and take actions across a sequence of steps. A retrieval failure early in that chain can send the entire workflow in the wrong direction. Vector search gives agents the semantic flexibility to find the right information at each step reliably, even as your data evolves.

Vector search is transformative, but even it has limits. Real enterprise knowledge bases contain a mix of structured data, precise identifiers, and rich narrative content. No single retrieval method handles all of these cases perfectly.

The most reliable production systems recognize this. They do not depend on vector search alone. They combine it with lexical search in a hybrid design that uses the strengths of both. That is where retrieval strategy becomes a genuine competitive advantage, and that is what we examine next.

What hybrid retrieval means for your AI applications

By now, you should see a pattern emerging. Lexical search is precise but brittle; it excels when the words match, and stumbles when they don't. Vector search is meaning-aware, but it can occasionally prioritize conceptual similarity over exactness in ways that matter.

Each approach has a role to play. And in the messy, language-rich environment of an enterprise, neither approach is sufficient on its own. This insight leads us to hybrid retrieval, which has become the common architecture for AI applications that must handle a wide variety of query types reliably.

Back to the customer service desk

Let's return one more time to our ecommerce company. The customer service assistant has been running for several months and handles thousands of interactions each day. The team has noticed something interesting in the data. Vector search dramatically improved resolution rates for open-ended, conversational queries. The frustrated customer asking about her missing package now reliably gets the right answer. But a new category of failure has emerged.

When customers reference a temporary promotional code such as, "*Why isn't promo code SUMMER25 working?*" the system occasionally struggles. Vector search is looking for semantic similarity, and there isn't much semantic meaning to extract from an alphanumeric code. These queries need exactness, not interpretation.

The team also notices that when customers ask nuanced questions that blend both types of need—"*Can I use SUMMER25 on the items in my delayed order?*"—neither approach alone handles it elegantly. The query has a precise component and a conceptual one, woven together in a single sentence.

This is where hybrid retrieval earns its place in the architecture.

Two engines, one result

A hybrid retrieval system runs both search methods in parallel. When a query comes in, the lexical engine scans for keyword and exact-term matches, producing a ranked list of results. Simultaneously, the vector engine converts the query into an embedding and finds the semantically closest content, producing its own ranked list. The system then combines these two lists into a single, unified candidate set, typically using a fusion algorithm such as **Reciprocal Rank Fusion (RRF)**, to merge the scores from each retriever. This fused set is then passed to a **reranker**, a cross-encoder model that jointly encodes the query and each candidate document to compute a fine-grained relevance score. Because the cross-encoder attends to the full interaction between query and document tokens, it can capture nuances that the initial retrievers miss, reordering the candidates so the most relevant results rise to the top. The reranked results are then passed to the language model.

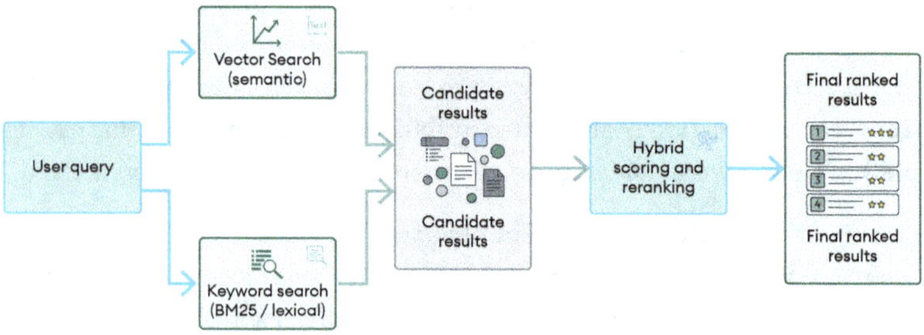

Figure 2.2 – How hybrid search combines vector search with lexical search

For our customer service assistant, hybrid retrieval closes the remaining gaps. The customer asking about a specific order number gets an exact match. The customer describing a frustrating experience in their own words gets a semantically relevant result. And the customer whose question spans both a promo code and a delayed order gets a result set that addresses the full complexity of their situation.

The effect on the RAG system is significant. When the retrieval layer consistently surfaces appropriate content regardless of query type, the language model has what it needs to generate accurate, grounded, and trustworthy responses. The system reduces the chance of failure and begins to feel more like something that understands, because the infrastructure beneath it now supports that illusion more effectively.

Optimizing search architecture for semantic relevance

Our e-commerce customer service assistant has come a long way. It started as a well-intentioned but brittle system that sent a frustrated customer information about shipping partners when she needed a refund. Now, it's a reliable, production-grade AI application that understands intent, handles precision queries, and combines the strength of multiple retrieval strategies to consistently surface the right information at the right moment.

That evolution didn't happen by accident. The team made deliberate architectural decisions at each layer of the retrieval stack that compounded into a trustworthy system.

Putting it all together

In production, retrieval architecture is not a single choice but a set of layered decisions. You decide which search methods to combine, how to weigh them, and how to tune them for your content and your users. Organizations that make these decisions have better search capabilities and AI applications that customers and employees are willing to depend on.

It's also worth being clear-eyed about trade-offs. Lexical search is mature, predictable, and relatively simple to implement and maintain, but it breaks down as language variability increases. Vector search is powerful and flexible, but it introduces additional infrastructure complexity, requires embedding models that need to be maintained, and can occasionally sacrifice precision for conceptual similarity in ways that matter. Hybrid retrieval delivers the best of both, but it comes with the combined weight of both systems to manage, tune, and scale.

For some organizations, this investment is clearly worthwhile. For others with simpler and more structured use cases, a well-tuned lexical system that evolves over time is a reasonable path. The most sophisticated design is not always the right one. The right architecture is the one that serves your users reliably within the constraints of your team.

As you evaluate which retrieval approach is right for your AI application, these are the questions worth considering:

- **How do your users naturally express their queries?**
  If they search with precise terminology, product codes, or structured identifiers, lexical search may serve you well. If they describe problems, ask questions, or use language that varies widely, vector search will be more resilient.
- **How consistent is the language in your knowledge base?**
  If your content is well-structured and terminology is standardized, lexical search can be highly effective. If documents were written by different teams over many years in different voices, vector search will bridge those gaps far better.
- **How much does exactness matter in your use case?**
  Customer service and internal knowledge applications tend to benefit from hybrid retrieval. Applications that surface regulatory content, contracts, or precise product data often can't afford the ambiguity that pure semantic search occasionally introduces.
- **How conversational is your AI application?**
  The more your users interact in natural language, the more your retrieval layer needs to understand intent rather than match keywords. Vector or hybrid search becomes increasingly important as interactions move away from structured queries.
- **How much does your content change?**
  If your knowledge base is relatively stable, a well-tuned lexical system may be sufficient. If policies, products, and procedures evolve frequently, vector search handles terminology drift far more gracefully because new language maps to the right meaning without requiring constant index maintenance.
- **What are your team's operational constraints?**
  The most technically sophisticated retrieval architecture is only an asset if your team can implement, maintain, and tune it effectively. Honestly assessing your team's capacity is just as important as assessing your users' needs.

These questions won't give you a single right answer, but they'll point you in the right direction and help you have a much more informed conversation with your technology teams and vendors.

Summary

Reliable AI doesn't begin with the language model but with the search layer underneath it. This chapter traced that idea through each evolution of retrieval technology, using a single customer service scenario to show how search quality determines the trustworthiness of every AI response built on top of it.

Lexical search offers speed and value when terminology is aligned, but it fails as soon as users describe problems in their own words. Embedding models addressed that failure by encoding semantic meaning into numerical representations. Vector search then used those representations to connect natural language queries to the right content, even when the words did not match. Finally, hybrid retrieval combined lexical and vector search. It preserved precision where exactness matters and semantic awareness where language varies.

No single approach is universally correct. The right retrieval architecture depends on how your users query, how your content is structured, how much precision your use case demands, and what your team can realistically maintain.

In the next chapter, we'll look at how MongoDB Atlas supports intelligent retrieval by combining operational data, vector search, and full-text search in a single platform. This unified approach helps cut down on system sprawl while keeping your data layer performant and easier to manage.

Search Fundamentals

Understand MongoDB Search, design search indexes, optimize search queries, and build efficient full-text search experiences.

`https://mdb.link/badge-search-press`

Vector Search Fundamentals

Build AI-powered search applications, create vector indexes, manage embeddings, and optimize retrieval strategies.

https://mdb.link/badge-vector-search-press

3

How MongoDB's Architecture Supports Modern AI

So far, we have covered how common AI architectures work and what they require. We've seen that many AI initiatives fail because the data infrastructure underneath them wasn't built to support what the model needs. When data is fragmented across multiple systems, even well-designed retrieval pipelines struggle to deliver consistent, reliable results in production.

That's where MongoDB comes in. As a unified data platform, MongoDB is built to support the full range of modern AI workloads without requiring you to manage a collection of disconnected, specialized systems. Its flexible document model stores the diverse data types that AI applications depend on together in a single record. And with vector search powered by Voyage AI's embedding and reranking models, MongoDB enables intelligent retrieval directly on that data, finding results by meaning rather than keywords, all within the same platform. In this chapter, we'll walk through the architectural capabilities that make that possible.

In this chapter, you'll learn:

- Why system sprawl undermines AI initiatives and how a consolidated data platform addresses it
- How MongoDB's document model stores diverse data types in a way that aligns with the needs of AI applications
- Understand how vector search, powered by Voyage AI, enables intelligent semantic retrieval natively within MongoDB

The case for unified data

Let's revisit the fictional insurance carrier example from *Chapter 1, Building a Unified Data Foundation for Sustainable AI Modernization*, where a regional carrier was attempting to deploy an AI agent to handle claims processing. Despite having capable models and experienced architects, their AI initiative stalled in production. Following a post-mortem analysis, the team identified three issues: data fragmentation, retrieval failures, and performance degradation under load.

To build their AI stack, they chose the best available tool for each job, which is what most organizations do. They utilized:

- A relational database for policy records and customer data
- A document store for claims notes and correspondence
- A dedicated vector database for embeddings
- An enterprise search engine for full-text retrieval
- A streaming platform to move data between all of them
- A layer of custom integration code to stitch it together into a coherent system

But what initially seemed like a modern data architecture ultimately compounded the problems they encountered. The appeal of assembling specialized tools is understandable as each one is genuinely good at what it does. But the moment you connect them into a pipeline, like the insurance carrier did, you inherit a new set of problems that none of them were designed to solve.

As this architecture grows, three common challenges emerge. First, **synchronization** becomes a persistent engineering burden, as every content update must correctly propagate across your embedding store, search index, and downstream caches in a timely manner. Second, **latency** begins to accumulate at every system boundary, leading to longer operation times in production. Finally, **operational overhead** multiplies with every system you add, as each has its own maintenance requirements. Together, these challenges mean that what starts as a straightforward integration can quickly evolve into a complex distributed system, where the cost of coordination can rival the cost of the core logic itself.

The compounding effect

What makes system sprawl particularly dangerous for AI initiatives is that the problems don't stay isolated. A synchronization delay in the embedding pipeline means the retrieval layer is working from stale data. When retrieval is stale, the language model reasons from outdated context. This outdated context results in incorrect responses. And an incorrect response in a customer-facing AI application can erode trust in the entire system. This is the compounding effect of fragmented infrastructure: a small failure in one layer quietly degrades the quality of every layer above it, often in ways that are difficult to trace back to their source.

Eventually, the architects at the insurance carrier reached the same conclusion that many teams eventually reach after dealing with a sprawling AI stack long enough: the complexity of managing the infrastructure had become a larger engineering burden than building the AI features themselves. Instead of accelerating their initiative, it was the thing slowing it down.

A better path starts with asking a different question. Instead of "*What is the best tool for each job*?" we should ask, "*What is the simplest architecture that can meet all of our requirements reliably*?" For most organizations building production AI today, that answer points toward consolidation.

Storing data in a way AI applications actually use it

If system sprawl is the problem, the document model is a significant part of the solution. But to understand why, it would help to first understand what made traditional data storage so poorly suited for AI in the first place.

Most enterprise databases were built around the relational model: tables, rows, columns, and strict schemas. This approach has served organizations well for decades because it is predictable, consistent, and excellent at answering structured questions about structured data. However, now the problem is that AI applications don't work with structured data alone. As we established in *Chapter 1*, the ability to manage diverse data types is one of the fundamental requirements for AI-ready infrastructure.

Think back to the insurance carrier's claims processing agent. A single claim requires a structured policy record, a free-form incident description, photographs, prior claim history, and vector embeddings for semantic search. In a relational architecture, that information lives across multiple tables or systems, forcing the agent to query each one, wait, and stitch the results together. But this is a structural mismatch as AI systems don't think in tables, they think in rich, multi-format context that must be assembled quickly and queried flexibly.

How the document model changes the equation

MongoDB's document model takes a fundamentally different approach that is designed to handle data diversity. Instead of forcing data into rigid rows and columns, it stores information in flexible, JSON-like documents that can contain whatever the application actually needs. So, whether it needs structured fields, nested objects, arrays, free-form text, references to images, or vector embeddings, all of these data types can be stored within a single record.

For the insurance carrier, this means that a single claim document can hold the policy details, the incident description, links to damage photos, the claimant's history, and the vector embeddings used for semantic retrieval in one place. Here is a simplified example of what it looks like in practice:

```
{
  "_id": "claim-00482",
  "policy_no": "AUTO-9842331",
  "status": "under_review",
  "claimant": {
    "id": "C102938",
    "name": "Marie Tremblay",
    "prior_claims": 1
  },
  "incident": {
    "date": "2026-02-14",
    "description": "Rear-ended at a stoplight. Significant
bumper damage.",
    "damage_photos": [
      "/claims/00482/photo_01.png",
      "/claims/00482/photo_02.png"
    ]
  },
  "coverage": {
    "liability": 1000000,
    "deductible": 500
  },
  "embedding": [0.0421, -0.1873, 0.9341, "..."]
}
```

A technical reader will recognize this as a standard MongoDB document. For everyone else, the key thing to notice is what *isn't* here: there are no foreign keys pointing to other tables, no joins required, no separate API calls to a vector store. The structured data, the free-form text, the photo references, and the semantic embedding all live together in one record. When the AI agent needs to process that claim, it issues one query to one system and reasons over the data as a unified whole. There is no orchestration across five platforms or waiting for synchronization.

Tip

If you're new to MongoDB, here's a quick orientation. In MongoDB, individual records are stored as **documents** , which are flexible, JSON-like objects that can hold structured fields, nested objects, arrays, and even vector embeddings, all in one place. Documents are grouped into **collections**, which are roughly analogous to tables in a relational database, except that documents in the same collection don't need to share the same structure. Collections, in turn, live inside a **database**. A single MongoDB deployment can host many databases, each containing many collections.

Flexibility that grows with your AI

Another dimension of the document model that is particularly valuable for AI initiatives is that it evolves without friction. AI applications are not static. The models, retrieval strategies, and data requirements all change as teams learn what actually works in production. In a relational system, every schema change is a project that requires migrations, downtime windows, and careful coordination across teams. In MongoDB's document model, new fields can be added to documents at any time, without touching existing records and without taking the system offline.

> **Note**
>
> Schema flexibility is one of MongoDB's most useful features, but flexibility doesn't mean structure is optional. Your schema can evolve without downtime, but you still need to model your data. In MongoDB, the way you structure your documents directly affects query performance, index efficiency, and how well your application scales. In a relational database, the schema enforces structure for you. In MongoDB, that responsibility shifts to the developer. The most important question to ask is: how will this data be accessed? Documents that are queried together should be stored together, and data that is always retrieved as a unit is a good candidate for embedding in a single document. Ignoring these best practices is one of the most common sources of performance problems in MongoDB deployments.

For the insurance carrier, this meant that when their team decided to start capturing a new type of data mid-production, they didn't need to redesign their database schema or schedule a maintenance window. They simply started including the new field in the relevant documents. This flexibility is a strategic advantage because organizations that can iterate quickly on their AI systems move faster than those whose infrastructure forces them to treat every change as a major engineering effort.

How vector search works in MongoDB

Storing data in the document model solves the fragmentation problem. Now, the system needs to be able to search it intelligently.

Consider what the claims processing agent needs to do every time a new claim arrives. It needs to find past cases that are *similar* to the current one, not cases that contain the same keywords, but cases that involve comparable damage patterns, related coverage scenarios, or analogous incident circumstances. A claim describing "*vehicle struck from behind at intersection with significant bumper deformation*" should surface when the agent is looking for precedents related to "*rear-end collision damage*," even though the two descriptions share almost no words in common.

That is the role of vector search. With MongoDB, vector search is a native capability that is powered by Voyage AI's state-of-the-art embedding and reranking models. It works directly on the data already living in your documents. Let's look at how this process works at a high level from start to finish.

Step 1: Creating and storing embeddings

Before MongoDB can search your data by meaning, that data needs to be translated into a form that captures what it means. That translation is the job of **vector embeddings**.

Remember, vector embeddings are numerical representations of data that capture meaning. When you pass your data through an **embedding model**, you get back an array of numbers (a vector) that represents the semantic meaning of that text. Texts with similar meanings produce vectors that land close together, even when they use completely different words.

The quality of your search results depends directly on the quality of the model generating your embeddings. A mediocre model produces mediocre coordinates, and no amount of clever querying can fix that downstream. This is one of the reasons why MongoDB acquired **Voyage AI**; to bring state-of-the-art embedding models, purpose-built for retrieval accuracy, directly into the platform. The models in Voyage AI consistently rank at the top of retrieval benchmarks and are designed from the ground up to capture the semantic relationships that matter most when finding relevant information.

You can generate embeddings using Voyage AI models built directly into the platform, or you can bring your own model and handle this process manually. However, when you use Voyage AI models, you gain access to the `autoEmbed` feature. With this feature, you can configure automated embedding at the database level, enabling MongoDB to handle embedding creation and keep embeddings in sync as your data changes. With this feature, you don't need to create custom pipelines or use external services.

Step 2: Creating a vector search index

Storing embeddings inside your documents is the first step. But to search across thousands or millions of embeddings efficiently, MongoDB needs a way to organize them for fast retrieval. That is the role of a **vector search index**.

Think of a vector search index as a map that helps MongoDB quickly navigate the high-dimensional "meaning space" where your embeddings live. Without it, every search would require scanning every single document in your collection and comparing embeddings one by one. The index gives MongoDB a structure to find the embeddings closest to a given query without exhaustively checking them all. By default, MongoDB Vector Search uses **Hierarchical Navigable Small World (HNSW)** graphs to organize embeddings, allowing the HNSW algorithm to quickly zero in on the most similar vectors by navigating through connected nodes rather than comparing against every embedding in the collection.

> **Note**
>
> A vector search index is different from standard database indexes you may already be familiar with. Standard indexes help MongoDB find documents based on field values, such as looking up a policy by its policy number. Whereas a vector search index helps MongoDB find documents based on the semantic similarity of their embeddings, such as finding past claims that are conceptually similar to a new one. Hence, both types of indexes can exist on the same collection, serving different query patterns.

Once the index is built, MongoDB keeps it updated as documents are added, modified, or removed. When a new record arrives and its embedding is written to the document, the vector search index incorporates it immediately. The next time your application searches for semantically similar content, that new record is already discoverable without any manual reindexing or pipeline orchestration.

Step 3: Querying data with $vectorSearch

With embeddings stored in your documents and a vector search index in place, the final piece is the query itself. In MongoDB, vector search queries are expressed through the **aggregation pipeline**, a framework that lets you process and transform data through a sequence of stages, where each stage performs a specific operation on the data flowing through it.

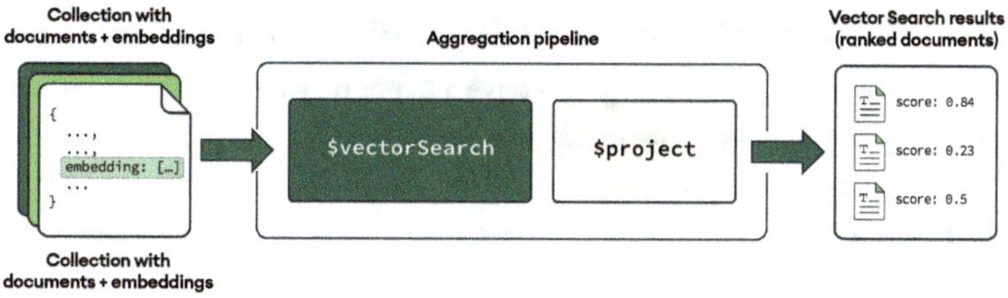

Figure 3.1 – An aggregation pipeline with $vectorSearch and $project stages

The `$vectorSearch` stage is where semantic retrieval occurs. It takes a query, either a query vector or raw text, and finds the documents whose embeddings are most similar. In plain terms, you are asking MongoDB: "*Find me the records that are closest in meaning to this.*"

This step relies on the same **embedding models** from Voyage AI that were used to create the stored embeddings in *Step 1*. When you pass a raw text query, MongoDB uses the Voyage AI model to convert it into a vector on the fly, then compares that vector against the indexed embeddings to find the closest matches.

MongoDB then evaluates a set of candidate documents internally and returns the top matches, ranked by how semantically similar they are to your query. Each result comes back with a relevance score that indicates how close the match is, so your application can see not just what was found, but how confident the match is.

And because `$vectorSearch` is part of the aggregation pipeline, it can be combined with other stages to sort or enrich the results all within the same query. You could, for example, add a filter to only consider records of a certain type, or add a stage to look up related information from another collection. The retrieval and the data processing happen together, in one place.

It is also worth noting that vector search is not the only retrieval capability MongoDB offers. MongoDB supports **lexical search** for precise keyword matching and **hybrid search** that combines vector and lexical results in a single pipeline. This means your application does not have to choose between understanding meaning and matching exact terms; it can use whichever approach best fits the query at hand.

Step 4: Refining results with reranking (optional)

With vector or lexical search, you receive a list of relevant results. But if your application requires absolute precision, you might consider adding a **reranking** step. This is a separate step from the ranking that happens during vector search itself, where MongoDB compares embeddings and returns results ordered by similarity.

A reranker takes the shortlisted results returned from your search query and evaluates each one alongside the original query to produce a more refined relevance ranking. Unlike the initial search, which encodes the query and documents independently, a reranker processes them together, allowing it to capture subtle relationships and nuances that may have been missed during the first pass. The outcome is a reordered set of results, with the most relevant documents surfaced at the top, not just the approximately relevant ones.

MongoDB provides access to Voyage AI's reranking models through the Atlas Embedding and Reranking API, currently in public preview, so this refinement step can be added without introducing a third-party service or leaving the Atlas ecosystem. These are distinct from the embedding models used in *Step 1*. While embedding models convert data into vector representations for search, reranking models are purpose-built to score the relevance of a query-document pair together. Voyage AI offers reranker models optimized for this task, delivering higher precision where it matters most.

Reranking is not necessary for every use case. For many applications, the results from a vector or hybrid search are more than sufficient. But in domains where precision is of utmost importance, such as legal, medical, financial, or compliance-sensitive workflows, a reranker can meaningfully improve the quality of your output by ensuring that the few, right documents rise to the top.

Summary

The insurance carrier's claims processing agent stalled not because the AI was inadequate, but because the infrastructure underneath it was fragmented across too many systems. This chapter showed how MongoDB eliminates that complexity through a set of capabilities that work together as a unified whole.

MongoDB's flexible document model stores structured fields, free-form text, image references, and vector embeddings together in a single record, managing the diverse data types that AI applications depend on without spreading them across separate systems. Change streams activate the claims processing agent the moment a new claim is submitted, fulfilling the third requirement for AI-ready infrastructure introduced in *Chapter 1*, and enabling timely, event-driven processing.

Once a claim is detected, the agent queries a single, composable aggregation pipeline that combines lexical search, vector similarity, metadata filters, and reranking in one place. Lexical search locks onto precise terms like medical procedure codes and standardized loss descriptions, while vector search, powered by Voyage AI's embedding models, surfaces semantically similar past cases based on meaning rather than keywords. A hybrid query runs both simultaneously, so the system returns documents that are precisely worded matches alongside those that are conceptually relevant. When precision matters most, the Voyage AI reranker reorders results so the most relevant precedents surface at the top.

The results come back with the full context the agent needs to act: complete claim documents enriched with relevance scores, all without leaving the database.

The result is an architecture where your AI application queries one system instead of many. Latency drops, consistency improves, and engineering effort shifts from managing infrastructure to building the features that create value.

In the next chapter, we will explore how MongoDB's replication and sharding architecture ensure that this foundation remains available, resilient, and ready to scale as your workloads grow.

Voyage AI with MongoDB

Generate and manage vector embeddings, apply Voyage AI models, build reranking pipelines, and optimize embedding strategies for performance and cost.

https://mdb.link/badge-voyage-ai-press

MongoDB Overview

Understand MongoDB architecture, explore the document model, design flexible schemas, and build scalable applications.

https://mdb.link/badge-overview-press

4

How Replication, Sharding, and Workload Isolation Keep AI Systems Running

In the previous chapter, we followed the story of an insurance carrier building a claims processing agent with MongoDB. That foundation solved the data architecture problem, but that is only part of the story.

A well-designed AI system also has to stay running when infrastructure fails, scale when the workload grows beyond what a single server can handle, and serve multiple customers without multiplying operational complexity. These are challenges that separate a promising pilot from a production system that the business can depend on.

In this chapter, you'll learn how to:

- Assess how MongoDB's built-in replication and automatic failover keep AI pipelines running when infrastructure fails
- Evaluate how horizontal scaling through sharding and dedicated Search Nodes allows AI systems to grow without rebuilding their foundation
- Understand how multi-tenant architecture patterns in MongoDB enforce data isolation at the database layer while serving many customers from a single platform

What replication and failover mean for business continuity

Let's take a look at a different kind of AI workload: a national freight and logistics company that has deployed a predictive maintenance agent across a regional fleet of 2,000 trucks in the Midwest. The system continuously streams in sensor data, such as engine temperature, vibration signatures, brake pad thickness, and tire pressure readings. The agent monitors this telemetry in real time, comparing incoming patterns against its knowledge base of historical failures to flag trucks that need attention before they break down on the road.

The system has been running for six months and has already prevented dozens of roadside breakdowns, but then, at 3 a.m. on a Thursday, the primary database node fails while the agent is mid-analysis on a batch of trucks flagged for potential brake system degradation. Sensor data is still streaming in from trucks on overnight long-haul routes.

In a fragmented architecture, this would be a crisis. With MongoDB, it's a non-event that's invisible to everyone else on the system. To understand why, let's take a closer look at how MongoDB handles failures under the hood.

How MongoDB approaches availability by default

MongoDB's answer to availability is built into its architecture from the ground up, rather than bolted on as an afterthought. Every production MongoDB deployment runs as a **replica set**, which is a group of database instances, typically three or more, that all maintain identical copies of the same data.

The **primary** node accepts all write operations and the remaining nodes, called **secondaries**, continuously replicate every change the primary makes, staying in sync in near real time. Think of it as a team of scribes, each copying every entry into their own ledger as it's written, so that if the lead scribe becomes unavailable, any one of the others can step in with a complete and current record.

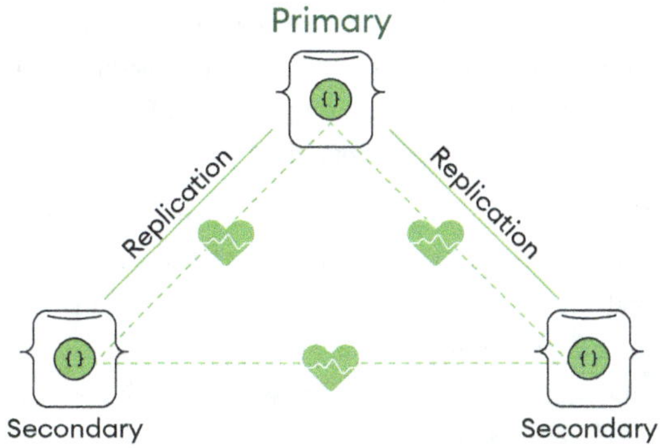

Figure 4.1 – A MongoDB replica set

If the primary node becomes unavailable, MongoDB's automatic failover takes over. The remaining members detect the failure through heartbeat signals exchanged between nodes every two seconds and hold an election to promote one of the secondaries to become the new primary.

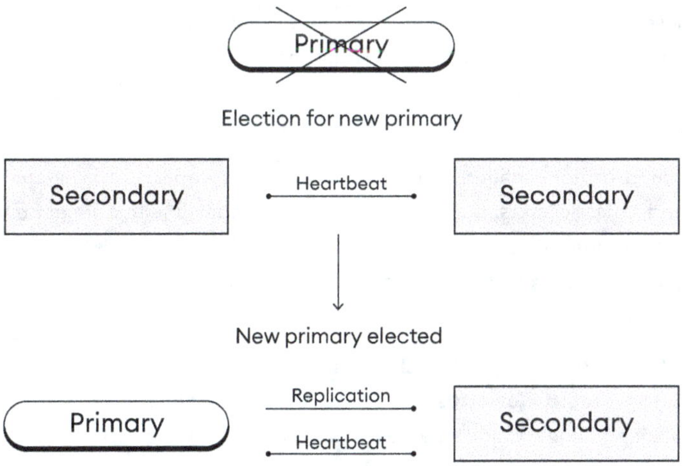

Figure 4.2 – Election for a new primary node

When configured correctly, this whole process completes in seconds, and from the application's perspective, the transition is largely invisible. MongoDB's drivers detect the change and route operations to the new primary, often retrying any writes that were in flight at the time of failure.

For the logistics company, a server failure during an overnight telemetry processing run is a brief, managed transition. The agent pauses for a moment, the replica set elects a new primary, and sensor analysis resumes. Trucks on long-haul routes continue streaming data, and the fleet manager's morning dashboard reflects every warning the agent identified overnight. The team doesn't have to manually intervene to prevent data loss.

Distributing availability across regions and clouds

For organizations with more demanding availability requirements or those operating in regulated industries where data residency and geographic redundancy are non-negotiable, MongoDB's replica sets can be distributed across multiple availability zones, regions, or even cloud providers. And for the logistics company, whose trucks cross state lines and time zones around the clock, this means that a regional cloud outage in one geography doesn't leave an entire corridor of the fleet without predictive maintenance coverage. The agent continues monitoring every vehicle, regardless of which data center went dark.

In a multi-region configuration, replica set members are placed in geographically separate data centers. If an entire region goes offline due to a cloud provider outage, a natural disaster, or a network partition, the remaining members in other regions can elect a new primary and continue serving the application without interruption.

MongoDB Atlas, MongoDB's fully managed cloud platform, takes this further by offering **multi-cloud clusters**, which are replica sets distributed across AWS, Azure, and Google Cloud simultaneously. This protects against provider-level outages, not just regional ones, and gives organizations the flexibility to meet data residency requirements without sacrificing availability.

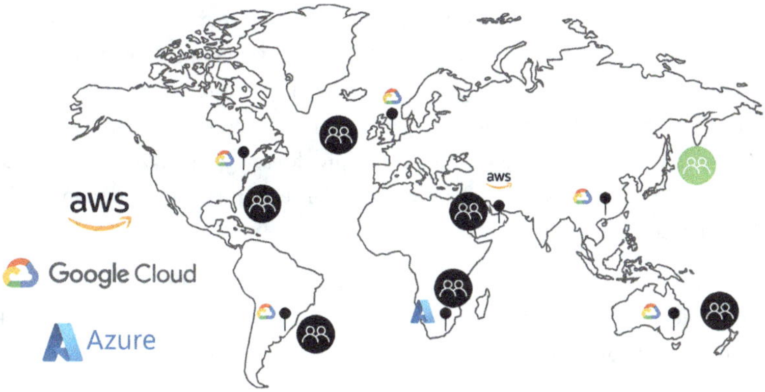

Figure 4.3 – A multi-region, multi-cloud cluster configuration

These configurations involve trade-offs, for example, distributing replica set members across regions introduces network latency between nodes, and multi-cloud deployments add operational considerations around provider-specific networking and cost structures. Not every workload justifies the added complexity. The right configuration depends on your availability requirements, your tolerance for latency, and the business consequences of an outage at each level of your infrastructure.

How sharding supports growing AI workloads

We've discussed how to manage and prevent a number of failure scenarios for our predictive maintenance agent, but what about success?

Imagine the predictive maintenance agent proves its value: breakdowns drop 40% in the first year, and the company estimates it has saved over $3 million in avoided roadside incidents, towing costs, and delivery delays. As a result, leadership decides to expand the system from a regional Midwest fleet to the company's full national fleet of 15,000 vehicles.

The knowledge base grows from thousands of maintenance records to hundreds of thousands. Previously, the vector index that fit comfortably in memory during the regional pilot is now straining the available RAM on a single server. Query latency, which had been measured in milliseconds, starts creeping upward as fleet managers run more concurrent searches such as, "*show me trucks with sensor patterns similar to the ones that preceded axle failures last winter.*" The team now finds themselves needing to scale the system.

The instinctive response to a performance problem is to make the server bigger by adding more RAM, upgrading the CPU, and provisioning more storage. This approach, called **vertical scaling**, is fast and simple. It requires no changes to your application code, and for many workloads, it buys meaningful headroom. But vertical scaling has a ceiling. Cloud providers cap the size of individual instances and for AI workloads specifically, the ceiling arrives faster than it does for traditional applications.

The sustainable answer is **horizontal scaling**: distributing the workload across multiple servers, so that each one handles a manageable share of the total load, and capacity can be added incrementally as demand grows.

How MongoDB sharding works

MongoDB's approach to horizontal scaling is called **sharding**. When a collection is sharded, MongoDB partitions its data across multiple servers, called **shards**, based on a field or combination of fields you designate as the **shard key**. Each shard holds a subset of the total data, and a routing layer called `mongos` sits in front of the cluster, consulting the cluster's config server to direct each query to the shard or shards that contain the relevant data.

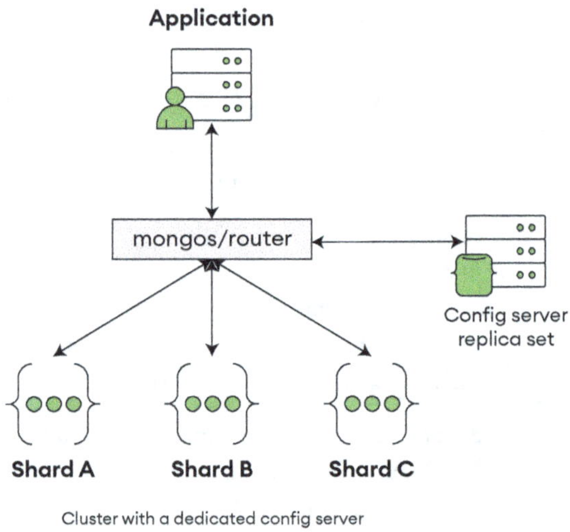

Figure 4.4 – High-level architecture of a sharded MongoDB cluster

From the application's perspective, this complexity is invisible. Your AI agent issues the same query it always has. The routing layer handles the rest by determining which shard to query, collecting the results, and returning them as if they came from a single system.

The practical effect is that both storage capacity and query throughput scale horizontally as you add shards. The logistics company's growing vector index, built from years of maintenance records, failure pattern analyses, and manufacturer bulletins, which had outgrown a single server, can be distributed across multiple shards, each holding a portion of the embeddings and handling a portion of the retrieval queries. As the fleet expands and telemetry history accumulates, additional shards can be added without taking the system offline and without rewriting the application.

Each shard in a MongoDB cluster is itself a replica set, which means the availability guarantees from the previous section extend across the entire sharded deployment. Sharding adds capacity; replication preserves continuity. The two mechanisms work together.

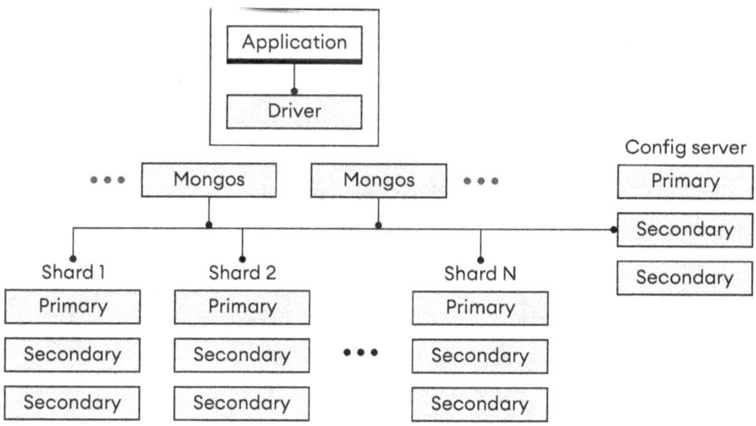

Figure 4.5 – Each shard is a replica set

Scaling Search independently of storage

While sharding addresses the raw capacity problem by distributing data across more servers, it does not solve every scaling challenge an AI workload creates. One of the more nuanced scaling challenges in AI applications is that search and storage workloads have different resource profiles. Storing and writing operational data is primarily a storage and I/O problem while running vector search queries at high concurrency is primarily a memory and CPU problem. In a traditional architecture, these two workloads compete for the same resources on the same nodes, which means tuning for one often degrades the other.

For the logistics company, this tension is inherent in the daily operation of the system. Thousands of trucks stream fresh telemetry data into the database around the clock. This creates a write-heavy ingestion workload that demands storage throughput and I/O capacity. At the same time, fleet managers run vector searches against historical failure patterns, which are memory and CPU intensive. Without workload isolation, a fleet manager's complex historical query could slow down the real-time ingestion pipeline that keeps the agent's view of the fleet current, or a spike in incoming telemetry could degrade the search experience for users querying the system.

MongoDB Atlas addresses this with **Search Nodes**, a dedicated infrastructure for Atlas Search and Vector Search workloads that can be scaled independently of the core database. When search demand spikes, for instance during a period of high claims volume, the search layer can be scaled up without touching the operational database nodes. When demand subsides, it can be scaled back down.

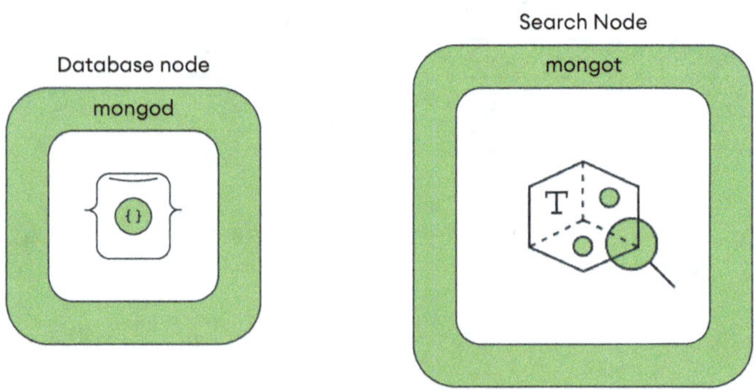

Figure 4.6 – Search Node independently scaling

This workload isolation has a meaningful impact on both performance and cost. For the logistics company, it means they are not permanently over-provisioning their entire cluster to handle peak search load, and the real-time ingestion pipeline never has to compete for resources with a sudden surge in queries.

In the next chapter, we'll discuss where Search Nodes fit into a larger performance strategy. For now, it's important to know that organizations that have adopted Search Nodes, like our logistics company example, report significant improvements in query latency and reductions in infrastructure spend because they are no longer over-provisioning their entire cluster to handle peak search load.

Summary

The logistics company's journey through this chapter illustrates how the decisions that matter most in production AI systems compound with one another. The document model eliminates transformation overhead by keeping sensor telemetry, maintenance records, and vector embeddings together in a single record. Replica sets and automatic failover keep the predictive maintenance agent running when infrastructure fails, completing recovery in seconds and protecting the stateful, in-progress work that AI agents depend on. Sharding distributes growing workloads across multiple servers so performance scales with the fleet without rebuilding the foundation. And dedicated Search Nodes separate the fleet manager's historical queries from the real-time ingestion pipeline, so neither workload has to compromise for the other.

What makes these capabilities powerful is that they are all properties of the same system. There is no synchronization tax between the telemetry store and the vector index, no separate failover procedure for the search layer, and no additional integration code to keep a dedicated vector database in sync with operational data. Replication preserves continuity, sharding adds capacity, and vector quantization keeps storage costs in check all on one platform to monitor, understand, and improve.

But resilience and scale are only part of the equation. A well-designed system also has to perform at the query latencies AI applications demand, without the hidden costs that accumulate when infrastructure is not purpose-built for the workload. That is where the next chapter begins.

Data Resilience: Atlas

Design resilient Atlas deployments, configure high availability, secure application data, and implement backup and recovery strategies.

https://mdb.link/badge-data-resilience-atlas-press

Data Resilience: Self-Managed

Design resilient self-managed deployments, configure replica sets, secure databases, and implement backup, recovery, and monitoring strategies.

https://mdb.link/badge-data-resilience-self-mng-press

Sharding Strategies

Design shard keys, implement sharded clusters, balance data distribution, and optimize horizontal scalability.

https://mdb.link/badge-sharding-press

5

Eliminating the Hidden Cost of AI Infrastructure with MongoDB

By now, you've seen how MongoDB brings together the features that make AI initiatives manageable. It uses a flexible document model that stores data the way your applications actually use it. It also provides a unified platform that eliminates the sprawl of stitching together multiple specialized systems. On top of that, its built-in availability and reliability help keep your pipelines running when things go wrong.

Those are the foundations. But a foundation alone doesn't make an AI system successful. It also has to *perform*.

Performance in AI systems isn't just about speed for its own sake. For example, when a fleet manager asks your predictive maintenance agent to surface trucks with particular brake patterns, they expect an answer in seconds not minutes. When that query takes too long, trust erodes. When it happens consistently, the system stops being used.

In this chapter, we'll return to the logistics company from *Chapter 4, How Replication, Sharding, and Workload Isolation Keep AI Systems Running*, and follow them through a very common challenge. Their vector search has slowed down, and they need to figure out why and what to do about it.

Along the way, you'll learn:

- How to diagnose the most common vector search performance problems
- How dedicated Search Nodes give your search workload the resources it needs without competing with the rest of your system

- How quantization can dramatically reduce the memory your vector indexes require
- How MongoDB views let you build leaner, more targeted indexes
- How to choose the right combination of these tools for your specific situation

Diagnosing vector search performance

The logistics company's predictive maintenance agent has been running well. Sensor data streams in from thousands of trucks around the clock, and fleet managers have come to rely on it. Then one morning, the team gets a notification that search is slow.

Queries that used to return in milliseconds are now taking seconds and fleet managers are noticing. The on-call engineer pulls up the monitoring dashboard and starts investigating.

This is a scenario that plays out regularly in teams running vector search in production. It's usually not a sign of a problem with the underlying infrastructure, but rather that the system has grown. The data has expanded, the index has become larger, and what worked at one scale is starting to strain at another.

For the logistics company, this means that the predictive maintenance agent that their fleet operations now depend on is at risk of becoming unreliable. Slow search doesn't just frustrate users; it undermines confidence in the AI system itself.

Why vector indexes demand so much memory

When vector search slows down, the most common culprit is that the vector search index no longer fits in memory. To understand this, let's briefly review how vector indexes are structured and why memory plays such an outsized role in keeping them fast.

Every document in your collection that has a vector embedding is represented as a list of floating-point numbers, one number per dimension. If you're using a model that produces 1,024-dimensional embeddings, each vector takes up roughly 4 kilobytes of space at standard precision. That might not sound like much, but multiply it across hundreds of thousands or millions of documents and the numbers add up fast.

On top of that, MongoDB's vector search uses a data structure called **hierarchical navigable small world** (HNSW) graph to make searches fast. You can think of it like a multi-layered map that lets the search engine navigate quickly to the most relevant results without checking every single document. That graph adds its own memory overhead on top of the raw vector data.

The vectors themselves and the HNSW graph together can easily push a mid-sized production collection well beyond the RAM available to the search process. The moment that happens, the search engine starts reading from disk instead of memory, and that's when latency becomes slow and unpredictable.

For vector search to be consistent and fast, the entire index needs to fit in the memory available to `mongot`, the search process that powers Atlas Search and Vector Search. When it doesn't, every query that has to reach out to disk pays a penalty that can compound under load.

> Note
>
> `mongot` is the background process that powers Atlas Search and Vector Search in MongoDB. Think of it as a dedicated search engine running quietly behind the scenes. It maintains your search indexes, listens for changes in your data, and handles every search query your application sends. When people talk about vector search being slow or an index not fitting in memory, mongot is the process feeling that pressure.

What to watch in MongoDB

The good news is that MongoDB makes it straightforward to see what's happening. A few key metrics tell most of the story:

- **System memory and search process memory**: Look at these together to assess whether mongot is under RAM pressure.
- **Search index size**: This tells you whether your indexes can realistically fit in available RAM.
- **Search page faults**: A high page fault rate confirms that slow queries are the result of disk reads happening on every step of the search.
- **Search normalized process CPU**: This catches a separate but related root cause, where indexing activity or your broader database workload is creating CPU contention.

You can set up alerts on these metrics directly in MongoDB Atlas, and if your team already uses a third-party monitoring tool, such as Datadog or Grafana, MongoDB integrates with those too, so you don't have to change the way you work to get visibility.

When the logistics company's engineer dug into the metrics, the picture became clear. The vector index had grown larger than the RAM available to `mongot`, and queries were hitting disk on every search. The index had simply outgrown the infrastructure it was running on.

The good news? MongoDB gives them three options to address it: dedicated Search Nodes, quantization, and optimizing vector search with views. Let's look at each one.

Co-located vs. dedicated Search Nodes

In *Chapter 4*, we introduced dedicated Search Nodes as a way to scale your search infrastructure independently of your database. But to understand why dedicated Search Nodes solve the logistics company's problem in this scenario, it helps to first understand what's happening in the default setup, where `mongod` and `mongot` run on the same nodes and why sharing resources can become a liability.

How the default setup works

By default, MongoDB runs two processes on the same nodes. `mongod`, which handles your operational data, such as reads, writes, and storage. And `mongot`, which powers your search indexes. This is called a co-located, or coupled, architecture.

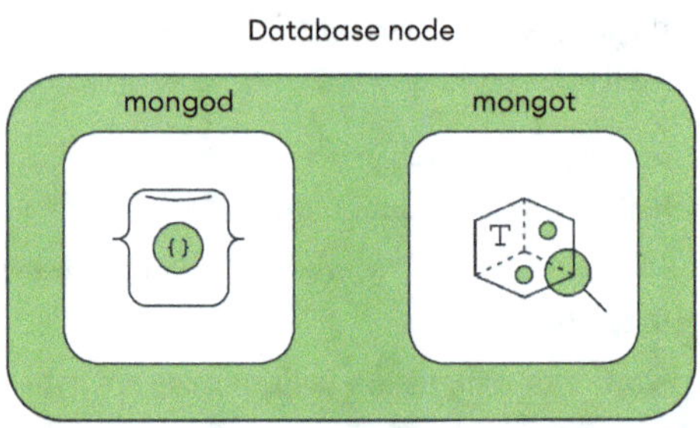

Figure 5.1 – Co-located nodes also known as a coupled architecture

In this setup, your operational workload and your search workload share the same pool of hardware resources including RAM and CPU. When both workloads are modest, that's perfectly fine. But when your vector index grows large enough to compete with your database for memory, you start to see the kind of slowdowns the logistics company is experiencing.

What dedicated Search Nodes change

With dedicated Search Nodes, `mongot` moves onto a completely separate, isolated infrastructure. Your operational cluster continues handling reads and writes, and your Search Nodes handle all your search needs. The two workloads no longer compete for the same resources.

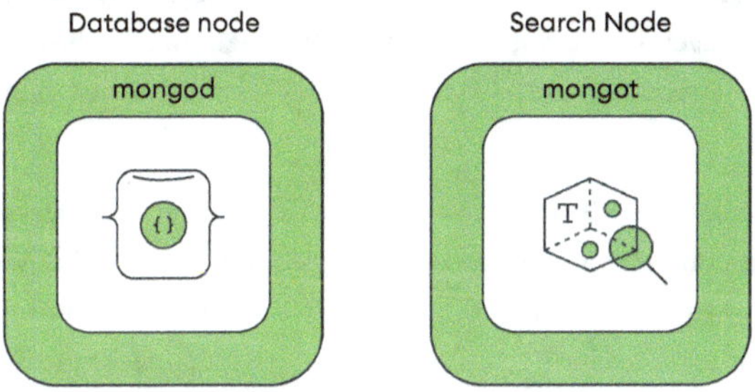

Figure 5.2 – A database node and a dedicated search node

The most immediate benefit is memory. On a dedicated Search Node, `mongot` isn't sharing RAM with WiredTiger, MongoDB's storage engine. Atlas Search Nodes allocate approximately 90% of node RAM to index data, with the remainder used by the search process itself. That's a dramatically larger and more predictable memory budget than `mongot` gets in a co-located setup.

And as we discussed in *Chapter 4*, you also gain the ability to size and scale your search infrastructure independently. You can add more search nodes to increase query throughput and lower latency. You don't have to over-provision your entire database cluster just to give `mongot` enough breathing room.

In addition, dedicated search nodes also unlock concurrent search, which allows `mongot` to search multiple parts of an index at the same time instead of one after another. The result is faster query responses, particularly for complex queries on large datasets, with no changes required to your application code.

For the logistics company, moving to dedicated Search Nodes is the most straightforward path to giving their vector index the memory it needs. It requires no changes to application code, just configuration and infrastructure sizing. Their fleet managers get fast, reliable search back. And the team gets a foundation that can grow with the fleet.

But dedicated Search Nodes aren't the only option for managing vector search resource costs. Let's look at two additional tools MongoDB provides: quantization and views.

Understanding quantization

Dedicated Search Nodes address the memory problem by giving `mongot` its own RAM budget, isolated from `mongod`. Quantization, on the other hand, is a technique that you can use to make the index smaller, rather than give it more room.

Quantization accomplishes this by reducing the number of bits used to represent each dimension value in your vectors. Remember those 4-kilobyte vectors we talked about earlier? Quantization changes their data type entirely in order to reduce the number of bits. The amount of RAM the index needs drops significantly, while the HNSW graph structure itself stays intact.

Think of the logistics company, storing the temperature readings from every truck in their fleet. They could record each reading to six decimal places, or they could round to the nearest whole number. They lose a tiny bit of precision, but the storage savings are significant and for most practical purposes, the rounded number is close enough to be useful.

Quantization works on the same principle. You're trading a small amount of precision for a meaningful reduction in memory requirements.

Two approaches: Scalar and binary

You can apply quantization in MongoDB Vector Search in two ways: automatic quantization and precomputed quantization.

With **automatic quantization**, you store raw float vectors in MongoDB as you normally would and add a `quantization` field to your index definition. `mongot` handles quantization at index build time, so you don't need to change your ingestion pipeline, and it works on existing collections immediately.

With **pre-computed quantization**, you quantize vectors before they ever reach MongoDB. The quantized vectors are stored directly in your documents, which reduces both the disk footprint in `mongod` and the RAM the index needs in `mongot`. We'll cover the specific packages and serialization format that make this possible when we implement that approach.

In addition to how you apply quantization, you also need to decide **which quantization type** to use. MongoDB Vector Search supports two types that differ mainly in how aggressively they reduce the size of your vectors.

Scalar quantization is the more conservative option. It reduces the precision of each dimension value—like rounding to fewer decimal places—while keeping the overall structure of the vector largely intact. The memory savings are meaningful, and the impact on search quality tends to be modest. Most teams find that scalar quantization maintains high recall, meaning the search still returns the results it should.

Binary quantization is more aggressive. It compresses each dimension value all the way down to a single bit, essentially a yes or no for each dimension. The memory savings are dramatic: binary quantization can reduce the memory footprint of a vector index by up to 96%. But that level of compression comes with a more significant precision trade-off. The reduced fidelity of the stored vectors can lower recall, causing the engine to miss some of the closest true matches to your query vector, meaning that your results may be less accurate.

To compensate, MongoDB includes an **automatic rescoring** step for binary quantization. After the initial search identifies the top candidates using the compressed vectors, MongoDB re-ranks those candidates using the original full-precision vectors before returning results to your application. This recovery step wins back most of the accuracy. In MongoDB's own tests, binary quantization with rescoring retained up to 95% search accuracy, meaning you lose very little result quality despite the aggressive compression. However, it's important to test whether the results meet the quality bar for your use case. Binary quantization might be the right approach for a product recommendation engine, for example, where near-accurate results are good enough and cost savings at scale matter, but not for medical record retrieval, where missing a relevant result could have serious consequences. For benchmark results and implementation details, see: `mongodb.com/blog/post/binary-quantization-rescoring-96-less-memory-faster-search`.

Automatic rescoring is only available when you use **automatic quantization.** If you use **pre-computed quantization,** MongoDB has no access to the original full-precision vectors, so it cannot perform this additional rescoring pass.

For the logistics company, quantization offers a way to reduce the memory footprint of their growing vector index without necessarily moving to a larger infrastructure tier. Scalar quantization is a reasonable first experiment because it is low risk, provides meaningful savings, and is easy to validate. Binary quantization is worth exploring if the memory pressure continues to grow, but it deserves careful testing before it goes anywhere near production.

Optimizing Vector Search with views

Dedicated Search Nodes give your search indexes more memory. Quantization makes the index smaller in memory. Views work differently from both: instead of changing the infrastructure or compressing the data, it changes *what gets indexed in the first place.*

What is a view

A view is a named, read-only query stored in MongoDB. When you create a view, you give it a name and define a pipeline, a series of steps that filter or transform documents from an underlying collection. MongoDB evaluates that pipeline on demand, for example, whenever someone queries the view or when `mongot` builds an index over it. The original collection is never modified.

If that sounds abstract, think of it as a window into your data. Instead of looking at the entire collection of products, a View lets you define a specific, filtered perspective on it, such as showing only recommended products. That's the perspective your vector index is built from.

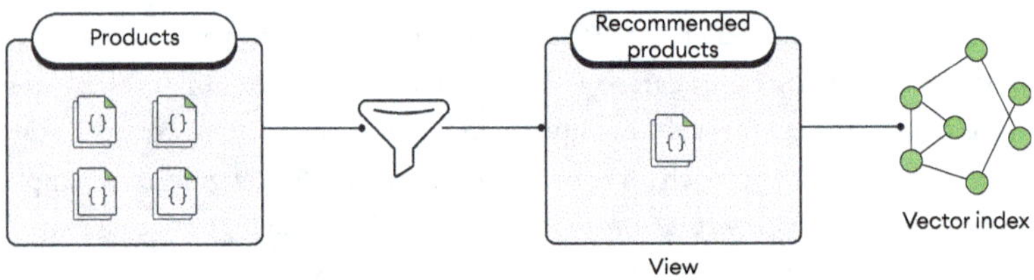

Figure 5.3 – A vector index is created from a view, containing only recommended products from a products collection.

Why this matters for Vector Search

Here's where it gets useful. When you create a vector index on a view instead of directly on a collection, `mongot` only indexes the documents the view produces. Whatever the view filters out never enters the HNSW graph at all.

For the logistics company, this is significant. Their collection contains sensor records for every truck in the fleet, including trucks that have been decommissioned, records that predate the current embedding model, and documents that were ingested before embeddings were added to the pipeline. None of those documents are useful for vector search. But without a view, they're all sitting in the index, consuming memory.

A simple view that filters to only documents with valid embeddings can meaningfully reduce the size of the index without touching the underlying data, without changing the application, and without any infrastructure cost.

Standard views vs. materialized views

MongoDB supports **one native view type** plus a **materialized view pattern**, and the difference matters for performance.

A **standard view** evaluates its pipeline fresh every time it's queried or every time `mongot` replicates index changes. This is lightweight and always current, but it works best when the pipeline is short and simple. Standard views support a specific set of pipeline stages for vector search indexing, including `$addFields`, `$set`, and `$match` with an `$expr` operator. If your pipeline needs anything beyond those, a standard view won't work for indexing purposes.

A **materialized view** in MongoDB is not a built-in feature but a **design pattern** in which you run an aggregation pipeline on a schedule (or in response to events), and write the results into a regular collection that your application and indexes read from. The pipeline cost is paid once at refresh time, not on every index replication event. This pattern is a good fit when your pipeline performs significant processing, such as multi-stage lookups, aggregations across large datasets, or transformations that rely on stages not supported for indexing in a standard view.

It's a good idea to start with a standard view when your filter is simple. Move to a materialized view when the pipeline complexity warrants it.

For the logistics company, a standard view is a natural first step. Filtering out documents without embeddings only requires a simple `$match` stage, exactly what standard views handle well. The index shrinks, memory pressure eases, and the change requires no infrastructure work and no application code changes.

As their understanding of the data matures, they can layer in more targeted filters, scoping the index to active trucks or to records from the current embedding model, and the view evolves with them.

Vector Search performance strategy

We've now covered three tools that MongoDB offers for addressing vector search performance: dedicated Search Nodes, quantization, and views. Each one solves the memory problem from a different angle. The natural next question is: how do you choose?

The honest answer is that most teams end up using all three. But they don't reach for them all at once, and they don't reach for them in the same order. Understanding the cost, risk, and effort profile of each one helps you sequence them sensibly.

Thinking about cost, effort, and risk

Dedicated Search Nodes carry the highest infrastructure cost of the three options, but they also carry the lowest engineering risk. There are no application code changes, no data pipeline modifications, and no quality trade-offs to validate. The work is in sizing and cost modeling, like figuring out which Search Node tier fits your workload and getting that line item scoped and approved. For teams with production latency requirements and indexes that are already straining available RAM, this is often the right first move precisely because it's the most predictable one.

Quantization shrinks the memory footprint of your index, which can delay or eliminate the need to move to a larger Search Node tier or reduce the cost of the tier you're already on. But the engineering effort varies significantly depending on which path you take. Automatic quantization is a moderate lift: you update the index definition and build a test plan to validate that recall hasn't degraded. Pre-computed quantization, where vectors are compressed before they reach MongoDB, is a much heavier change that touches your ingestion pipeline, your driver code, and your query layer. Either way, quantization is lossy, and the quality risk is real. If you don't validate recall carefully, you can ship a degraded search experience without realizing it.

Views are the lightest option from an infrastructure and engineering perspective. A simple filter requires minimal code and no infrastructure changes. The risk is in getting the filter right: too aggressive and you exclude documents that should be searchable; too permissive and you don't get the memory savings you were hoping for. Using unsupported pipeline operators in a standard view can leave your index in a stale state, so it's worth understanding the constraints before you build.

Approach	Infrastructure cost	Engineering effort	Quality risk
Dedicated Search Nodes	Highest	Low	None
Automatic quantization	Lower	Moderate	Real
Pre-computed quanization	Lower	High	Real
Views	Lowest	Low	Low

Table 5.1 – A comparison of dedicated search nodes, automatic quantization, pre-computed quantization, and views.

When to reach for each one

Start quantization experiments early before you need them. The worst time to discover that binary quantization drops recall by 15% is during a production incident. Run tests on staging indexes during the planning and development stages, while there's time to evaluate the results carefully. If quantization is viable for your workload, you'll have the data to back the decision when it matters.

Treat dedicated Search Nodes as a first-class option for key workloads, not an afterthought. If vector search is in the critical path of your application and your indexes are expected to grow to several gigabytes, factor Search Nodes into your production design from the start. The contention and resource pressure problems we've covered are much harder to address after users are already feeling them.

Let views evolve with your understanding of the data. Start simple and filter out documents without embeddings, and see how much that moves the needle. Then layer in more targeted filters as your domain model matures. Views are easy to update, and the index rebuilds automatically when you do.

For the logistics company, the path forward combined all three. They started with a standard view to exclude decommissioned trucks and pre-embedding records, which brought the index size down meaningfully. They enabled scalar quantization on the updated index and validated recall against their staging environment. And they factored dedicated Search Nodes into their next infrastructure planning cycle, knowing the fleet and the index would keep growing.

The result was a predictive maintenance agent that performed reliably again, on infrastructure the team understood and could continue to tune as the system scaled.

Summary

In this chapter, we followed the logistics company through one of the most common challenges teams face when vector search moves into production: the index outgrows available memory and performance becomes unpredictable.

We explored three tools MongoDB provides to address it. Dedicated Search Nodes isolate your search workload onto its own infrastructure, giving `mongot` a large, predictable memory budget without competing with your operational database. Quantization compresses your vector embeddings to reduce the memory your index requires, with scalar quantization offering a low-risk starting point and binary quantization delivering more dramatic savings for workloads that can absorb the trade-off. Views let you build leaner, more targeted indexes by controlling exactly which documents enter the HNSW graph.

These techniques aren't mutually exclusive. The teams that manage vector search performance most successfully treat all three as part of their toolkit, reaching for each one at the right moment.

But speed and reliability are only part of what it takes to operate AI systems responsibly at scale. In the next chapter, we'll look at the other side of that equation: how to govern who can access your data, how to protect it, and how to ensure that every decision your AI system makes can be traced, explained, and defended.

Vector Search Performance

Analyze vector search performance, diagnose bottlenecks, optimize vector indexes, and tune deployments for scalability and efficiency.

https://mdb.link/badge-vector-perf-press

Vector Search Fundamentals

Build AI-powered search applications, create vector indexes, manage embeddings, and optimize retrieval strategies.

https://mdb.link/badge-vector-search-press

6

Governance and Compliance for AI-Ready Organizations

Over the course of this book, we've covered a lot of ground. You've seen how MongoDB's flexible document model stores the diverse data types that AI applications depend on. You've seen how a unified platform eliminates the sprawl of stitching together multiple specialized systems. You've followed the logistics company as they diagnosed and resolved vector search performance challenges, and you've seen how replication, sharding, and workload isolation keep AI systems running when things go wrong.

Architecture, performance, availability, and scale form the foundation of a production-ready AI system. But there is one more important piece we haven't addressed yet: security and governance.

Without clear governance, even a well-architected AI system can expose sensitive data, violate regulatory requirements, or erode the trust your organization has spent years building. These risks multiply as you scale.

In this chapter, you'll learn:

- Why governance and compliance requirements need to be established before AI systems go into production
- How MongoDB's built-in governance capabilities protect your data at the platform level
- Why observability is essential for operating AI systems responsibly at scale
- How multi-tenant architecture patterns enforce data isolation while serving multiple customers or business units from a single system

Defining your governance requirements

Organizations operating under strict regulations already have governance policies in place. They know how to handle sensitive data, manage access, and meet compliance requirements. What's less familiar is applying those policies to an AI system that makes decisions autonomously, retrieves data at machine speed, and operates across boundaries that human workflows never crossed.

Consider a fictional legal services firm that has just approved an initiative to build an AI assistant to help attorneys research case law, surface relevant precedents, and draft document summaries. Before a single line of code is written, the firm is working through its governance requirements deliberately, so that when development begins, the right guardrails are already defined.

The firm already has strong governance practices: policies for how client data is handled, who can access what, and how sensitive information is protected. What they're working through now is how those existing commitments apply to an AI system. That's where things get interesting, because AI introduces questions that traditional governance frameworks weren't designed to answer.

When a human attorney accesses a client file, there's a clear chain of accountability. When an AI system retrieves documents autonomously, potentially across hundreds of matters in seconds, that same accountability needs to exist, but the mechanisms look different.

The questions this firm is asking are the same ones any organization should ask before an AI initiative moves into development:

- What data will the AI system access, and where does it come from?
- Who is authorized to query it, and under what circumstances?
- How will the organization trace what the system surfaced if a client or regulator ever asks?
- What happens if the AI retrieves a document from the wrong matter, and how will they know?

For a law firm, client confidentiality is both a professional and legal obligation. If the AI surfaces documents from one client matter in response to a query about another, the consequences can include compliance violations that threaten the firm's reputation and its fundamental duty to its clients.

The same principle holds across industries. Without a clear handle on data lineage, such as who generated the data, where it lives, and how it moves through your systems, deploying AI on top of that data introduces risk your existing governance framework may not yet account for. When you scale generative AI across an enterprise, any gap in those answers gets amplified.

Getting governance right before go-live is far less costly than revisiting it afterward.

For this firm, that means defining requirements before a single attorney queries the system: role-based access controls, matter-level permissions, encryption at rest and in transit, query logging for an auditable retrieval trail, and ongoing runtime visibility into what the AI is actually doing.

Let's look at how MongoDB addresses each of these requirements.

Controlling access and protecting data

MongoDB includes core governance capabilities built directly into the platform. For organizations running AI initiatives on sensitive data, three capabilities matter most: **role-based access controls** (**RBAC**), permissions management, and encryption. Let's walk through each one and see what they would have meant for the legal services firm.

Authentication and RBAC

RBAC lets you define exactly which users, roles, and services can access specific data and what they're allowed to do with it. Instead of granting broad access and hoping people use it responsibly, you create roles that map to real job functions and assign only the permissions each role actually needs.

In the context of AI, this matters because an AI agent doesn't exercise judgment about whether it should access a particular document; it accesses whatever it has permission to access. That makes the role and permissions you assign it one of the most consequential governance decisions you'll make.

MongoDB supports multiple authentication mechanisms, including **salted challenge response authentication mechanism** (**SCRAM**), x.509 certificates, and **lightweight directory access protocol** (**LDAP**). For AI systems, service accounts are the recommended approach. Every agent authenticates with a dedicated, auditable identity rather than a shared or human credential. Once that identity is established, RBAC determines exactly what it can see and do at the database level. You can define roles that grant read-only access to one collection, read-write access to another, and no access at all to a third. Those rules apply equally to human users and application-level service accounts.

For the legal services firm, this means the research assistant can be scoped to access only the matter files relevant to a given attorney's active cases. Privileged communications, opposing counsel documents, and unrelated client files remain completely off-limits because the role doesn't permit them.

Permissions management

RBAC defines what roles can do. Permissions management is how you operationalize those roles as the organization grows and changes.

In practice, this means being able to create, modify, and revoke roles and privileges, and doing so at a level of granularity that matches the complexity of your data. MongoDB supports permissions at the database level, the collection level, or scoped to specific actions such as `find`, `insert`, and `aggregate`, allowing you to be as precise as your governance requirements demand.

As the firm takes on new practice areas or expands to offices with different regulatory obligations, distinct roles can be defined for each context.

Encryption and data privacy

RBAC and permissions management control who can access data. Encryption ensures that even if data is intercepted or improperly accessed, it remains unreadable.

This matters especially when AI systems pull in content from external sources. Court filings, third-party discovery materials, scanned records, and any other document entering the retrieval pipeline from outside the firm's own systems must be vetted for privacy considerations before the AI can surface it.

MongoDB supports encryption at rest and in transit, ensuring data is protected whether it's stored in the database or moving between systems. For the legal services firm, this means client documents are protected end to end throughout the retrieval pipeline so that AI can do its job while maintaining confidentiality.

Together, these three capabilities give organizations a governance foundation that works at the speed AI demands. Access is controlled before data is ever surfaced, data is protected end to end through encryption, and permissions can evolve alongside the business without creating gaps or requiring a rebuild.

Auditing and observability

Access controls and encryption determine what your AI system is allowed to do and protect the data it touches but they don't tell you what the system actually did. That's the role of observability: giving organizations the ongoing visibility to operate AI responsibly, catch problems before they become incidents, and demonstrate accountability to clients and regulators.

Observability is also where the audit trail lives, a structured record of what the system saw, what it decided, and why. For regulated industries in particular, that record can be legally consequential. When a decision gets challenged, you need to reconstruct the reasoning behind it, not approximate it after the fact. Without observability, you cannot know whether your AI is working correctly, and you cannot prove to anyone outside your organization that it is.

The black box problem

Unlike traditional software, which tends to announce its failures, AI agents can fail silently, producing fluent, confident-sounding answers while getting things wrong. Without deliberate observability, everything between input and output is invisible. You see what went in, and you see what came out. Everything in between is a black box.

That invisibility is what makes traditional monitoring insufficient on its own. Traditional monitoring asks questions you already know to ask: Is the server up? Is the error rate above 5%? Observability, on the other hand, is about building systems that can answer questions you didn't anticipate. For AI agents, that means being able to ask: why did the system surface that document? Why did the agent make that recommendation? Where in the workflow did the answer go wrong?

When an AI agent produces a wrong answer, the cause could be any of the following:

- The agent reasoned incorrectly (a model problem)
- A tool the agent called returned stale or irrelevant data (a data problem)
- The wrong documents were retrieved as context (a retrieval problem)
- The underlying infrastructure was slow or overloaded (an infrastructure problem)

Without observability these causes are indistinguishable, meaning that every fix requires guesswork.

The three signals

Effective observability for AI systems relies on three types of signals working together.

Logs capture a timestamped record of what happened at every step: which data was accessed, which tools were called, what the agent did, and what it returned. For AI systems, logs are also the foundation of your access audit trail, capturing which user or process initiated a request, which documents were retrieved, and whether any access boundaries were approached. MongoDB's auditing capabilities feed directly into this layer, capturing authentication events, queries, and data modifications in a structured format that compliance teams can query and trace. For the legal services firm, if a client questions what information was used to prepare their matter or a conflict-of-interest concern arises, the audit log is the record that answers that question.

Metrics are quantitative health signals over time, such as response rates, error rates, and latency trends. They help you determine whether the system is performing as expected and alert you when something drifts.

Traces capture the end-to-end journey of a single request through the system, showing exactly where a failure occurred in a multi-step workflow. For regulated industries, traces also serve as compliance evidence, documenting what the agent accessed, in what order, and why.

Together, these three signals give the legal services firm's leadership a complete picture: a traceable record of what the AI accessed, and the ongoing confidence that it's behaving as intended. If an attorney questions why a particular precedent was included in a research summary, the answer is in the logs. If the system starts drifting outside its authorized scope, the metrics and traces are there to catch it.

Observability is the operational foundation that makes AI systems trustworthy, auditable, and improvable over time. Without it, you cannot know whether your AI is working correctly and you cannot demonstrate to clients, regulators, or your own leadership that it is.

Multi-tenancy

The legal services firm's governance story so far has been about one firm protecting its own clients' data. But what happens when the firm's success with AI-assisted research attracts attention and a legal technology company approaches them about licensing the platform to other firms?

Suddenly the question changes. It's no longer just: how do we protect our clients' data? It becomes: how do we build one system that serves multiple law firms, each with their own clients, matters, and confidentiality obligations, without letting one firm's data ever reach another's?

This is the multi-tenancy problem, and it's one of the most consequential architectural decisions you'll face when scaling AI systems.

What multi-tenancy means

You can think of multi-tenancy as an apartment building. Every tenant lives under the same roof and shares the same infrastructure, such as the plumbing, the electrical system, and the elevators. But each apartment is a private, self-contained space. You don't walk into your neighbor's unit, and they don't walk into yours. The building is shared; the living spaces are not.

Multi-tenant software architecture works the same way. Multiple customers, or tenants, share the same application and the same database infrastructure, but each tenant's data is logically isolated from every other tenant's data. Done well, this gives you the operational efficiency of running one system instead of many, while still enforcing the strict data separation that governance and compliance demand.

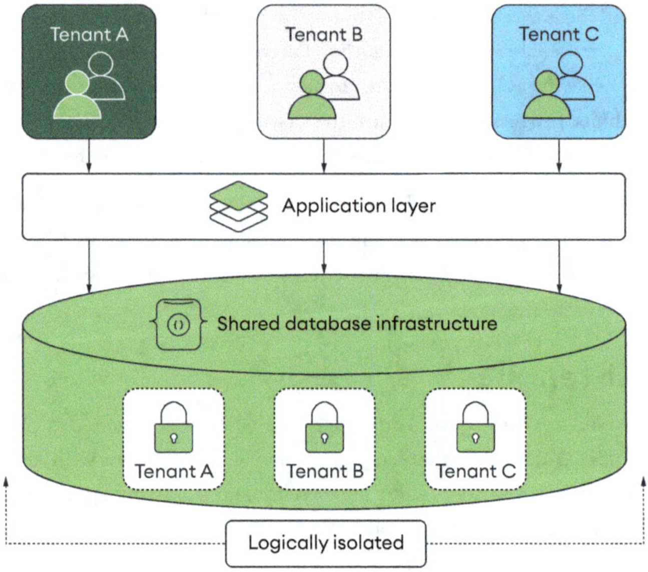

Figure 6.1 – Multi-tenant architecture

Without multi-tenancy, the alternative is to deploy a completely separate instance of your application and database for every customer. That approach guarantees isolation, but it also multiplies your operational burden. Multi-tenancy solves this by keeping the infrastructure consolidated while enforcing isolation at the data layer.

How MongoDB keeps tenant data separate

In MongoDB, multi-tenancy is typically implemented by including a tenant identifier in every document. Queries are always scoped to a specific tenant, so one customer's data is never returned in another customer's results. This approach keeps all tenants in the same collection, which simplifies operations, while the tenant identifier acts as the boundary that keeps data isolated.

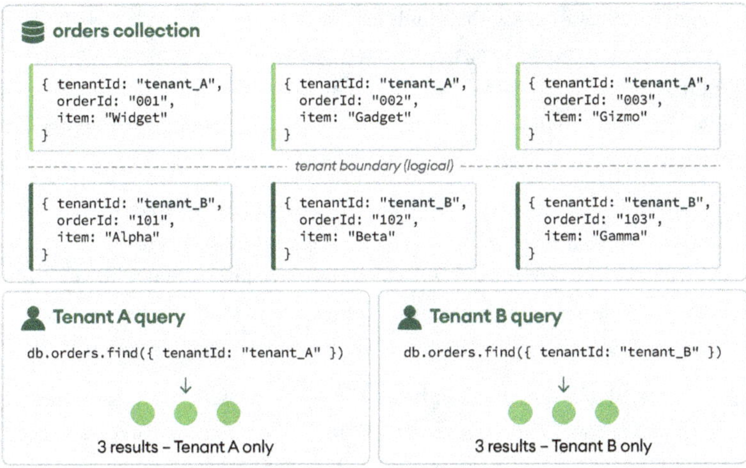

Figure 6.2 – Queries scoped to a specific tenant

For the legal platform, this means that when an attorney at Firm A queries the research assistant, it only ever surfaces documents from Firm A's matters. Firm B's case files are in the same collection, on the same infrastructure but completely invisible to any query that doesn't carry Firm A's identifier.

Flat indexes

Keeping tenant data logically separate is one challenge. Making sure your search infrastructure respects those boundaries efficiently is another. You can scope every query to a specific tenant, but if the underlying index was built without tenancy in mind, the search engine still has to search across every tenant's data before narrowing down to the one that matters.

The challenge is that the most common index type for vector search, the HNSW graph discussed in *Chapter 5, Eliminating the Hidden Cost of AI Infrastructure with MongoDB,* was designed for searching large, shared datasets. It builds a connected map of all the vectors in the collection and navigates that map to find the closest matches. This works beautifully when you're searching across the entire dataset, but in a multi-tenant application, searches are almost always limited to a single tenant's data. As a result, the HNSW graph ends up doing unnecessary work by navigating through vectors that belong to other tenants, which will ultimately be filtered out before results are returned.

MongoDB addresses this with flat indexes. Unlike HNSW, a flat index doesn't build a navigational graph. Instead, it performs a direct comparison against the vectors that match your filter, in this case, the tenant identifier. For small-to-moderate tenant datasets, this is faster and more efficient than navigating a shared HNSW graph and then discarding most of the results.

Flat indexes are the right choice when your tenants have relatively small vector datasets, and your queries always include a tenant filter. As tenant data grows larger, HNSW with pre-filtering may become more efficient, but for many multi-tenant applications, including the insurance carrier's platform, flat indexes offer the best combination of performance, simplicity, and tenant isolation.

For the legal platform, flat indexes allow the firm to scale from serving one organization to serving many, all on the same infrastructure without compromising the matter-level isolation that client confidentiality demands.

Summary

Security, governance, observability, and multi-tenancy are layers that, when working together, ensure that AI systems handle sensitive data in ways that are authorized, traceable, and trustworthy.

In this chapter, we followed a fictional legal services firm through the governance decisions that must be made before an AI system goes into production. Before a single line of code was written, the firm was already defining access controls, encryption requirements, audit obligations, and data boundaries, ensuring the right guardrails were in place from the start.

We explored how MongoDB's built-in capabilities support that foundation. RBAC ensures that the AI can only reach authorized matter files. Encryption protects client documents throughout the retrieval pipeline. Through logs, metrics, and traces, observability gives the firm ongoing visibility into whether the system is behaving as intended.

We then examined what happens when that system scales to serve multiple firms. MongoDB's multi-tenant architecture patterns enforce data isolation at the data layer, making it possible to serve many clients from a single system without compromising the confidentiality obligations each one carries.

A few best practices are worth keeping in mind as you work through the same decisions for your own organization:

- **Start with policy.** Review and define your governance framework before configuring a single access control rule.
- Treat AI systems as first-class participants in your access model. Every agent should authenticate with a scoped role.
- **Encrypt sensitive data.** Data privacy obligations don't pause simply because an AI system is accessing the data. Encryption at rest and in transit is important for organizations with strict governance and compliance policies.
- **Log everything the AI touches.** Autonomous systems make decisions at a speed and scale that humans can't manually review in real time. Comprehensive audit logging is how you maintain accountability.
- **Monitor AI behavior, not just infrastructure.** Observability is how you catch governance failures before they become compliance incidents.
- **Design for multi-tenancy early if you anticipate growth.** Retrofitting matter-level or client-level isolation into a system that wasn't designed for it is significantly harder than building it in from the start.

Security, governance, and observability are not features you add at the end. They are design decisions that shape how much your organization and your clients can trust the AI systems you build.

Encryption at Rest

Configure encryption at rest, integrate customer-managed encryption keys (BYOK), and secure data with external key management systems.

https://mdb.link/badge-encryption-at-rest-press

Glossary

Aggregation pipeline: A sequence of stages used to process, filter, transform, and enrich data in MongoDB. Because aggregation pipelines allow `$vectorSearch`, sorting, and filtering to work together within a single pipeline, AI applications can retrieve and process data in a single query rather than across multiple disconnected systems.

AI agent: An autonomous system that perceives its environment, reasons through multi-step tasks, and takes action to accomplish goals without step-by-step human instruction. Unlike a simple chatbot, an agent can coordinate tools, call external services, and manage complex workflows, making reliable, unified data infrastructure critical to its performance.

AI pipeline: The connected series of steps through which data flows to power an AI application, from ingestion and storage to retrieval, model inference, and response. A failure at any stage, such as stale embeddings or a database outage, can degrade the quality or availability of the entire system.

Automatic failover: A mechanism that detects when a primary database node has become unavailable and automatically promotes a secondary node to handle write operations. MongoDB implements this through a consensus-based election among the remaining nodes. This transition typically completes within seconds, keeping AI systems running without manual intervention.

Change stream: A real-time data streaming capability that allows applications to subscribe to and respond to changes in a database, such as inserts, updates, or deletes, as they happen. MongoDB offers native change stream support. For AI systems, this enables event-driven processing such as triggering an agent workflow the moment a new claim or record arrives.

Data lineage: The documented record of where data originated, how it has moved through systems, and what transformations it has undergone. In AI applications, understanding this history is essential for tracing retrieval results, meeting compliance requirements, and ensuring sensitive records do not reach pipelines where they are not authorized.

Dedicated Search Node: A node in MongoDB Atlas allocated exclusively to Search and Vector Search workloads, separate from the nodes that handle operational reads and writes. This prevents memory-intensive vector indexes from competing with application data for resources, improving both search performance and overall system stability.

Document model: MongoDB's core data structure, in which each record is stored as a self-contained, flexible document that can hold structured fields, unstructured text, arrays, and vector embeddings together. This eliminates the need to spread diverse AI application data across multiple specialized systems.

Embedding model: A machine learning model that converts content such as text, images, or structured records into a numerical vector representation. The quality of the model directly influences latency and how accurately a retrieval system can find semantically related content in response to a query.

Encryption at rest: A security control that encodes stored data so it cannot be read without the appropriate decryption key. When combined with encryption in transit, it ensures that sensitive information remains protected throughout its lifecycle.

Flat index: A vector index type that performs a direct comparison against a pre-filtered set of documents rather than navigating a shared graph structure. It's well-suited for multi-tenant applications where every query is scoped to a single customer's data, avoiding the overhead of scanning irrelevant records from other tenants.

Hierarchical Navigable Small World (HNSW) graph: The default data structure that powers MongoDB's vector indexes. It organizes vectors into a multi-layered map that lets the search engine navigate quickly to the most relevant results without comparing every document in the collection.

Hallucination: A response generated by a large language model that sounds plausible but is factually incorrect or fabricated. This occurs when the model fills gaps in its knowledge with confident-sounding approximations rather than verified information. Grounding responses in retrieved, trusted data—as RAG systems do—significantly reduces the likelihood of this behavior.

Hybrid search: A search strategy that runs lexical and vector search simultaneously, and then combines their results into a single ranked list. This allows an AI system to handle both precise queries and open-ended semantic questions within the same pipeline without sacrificing accuracy in either case.

Knowledge base: A curated collection of documents, records, or structured data that an AI system draws on to answer questions or complete tasks. In a RAG system, the retrieval layer queries this collection to surface content relevant to the user's input before the language model generates a response.

Large language model (LLM): A machine learning model trained on vast amounts of text that can understand and generate human language. LLMs are capable reasoners and communicators, but their knowledge is fixed at training time and excludes proprietary data, which is why they are commonly paired with a retrieval layer.

Lexical search: A technique that matches queries to documents based on exact or near-exact word matches. Also called keyword search, it is fast and reliable for precise identifiers like order numbers or codes, but can miss relevant results when users phrase questions differently from how the content is written.

Multi-tenancy: An architectural pattern in which a single system serves multiple customers, called tenants, while keeping each tenant's data logically isolated from all others. In MongoDB, this is typically implemented by including a tenant identifier in every document and scoping all queries so that one customer's data is never returned in another's results.

Observability: The ability to understand what an AI system is doing internally by examining its logs, metrics, and traces. For AI systems, it provides the audit trail needed to determine what data an agent accessed, what decisions it made, and whether its behavior stayed within authorized boundaries.

Quantization: A technique that compresses vector data into a more compact format to reduce the memory a vector index requires.

Recovery point objective (RPO): The maximum amount of data loss, measured in time, an organization can tolerate if a system failure occurs. AI systems with a low RPO rely on continuous replication to ensure that only a few seconds of data at most would be unrecoverable after an outage.

Recovery time objective (RTO): The maximum length of time a system can be offline before business operations are meaningfully impacted. AI workloads with a low RTO depend on automatic failover and built-in redundancy to restore service in seconds rather than hours.

Replica set: A group of MongoDB database instances, typically three or more, that each maintain identical copies of the same data. When one node fails, the group automatically selects a new primary so that reads and writes can continue without manual recovery or data loss.

Reranking: An optional step in the retrieval process that takes an initial set of candidate results and reorders them using a reranking model to better reflect the intent of the query. Improving the quality of retrieved content before it reaches the language model directly improves the accuracy and usefulness of the final response.

Retrieval-augmented generation (RAG): A technique that combines a large language model with a retrieval system to ground AI responses in actual, current data. Instead of relying solely on what the model learned during training, a RAG system retrieves relevant documents from a knowledge base at query time and provides them as context before a response is generated.

Role-based access control (RBAC): A security model that grants data access permissions based on predefined roles rather than individual identities. In AI systems, it ensures that automated agents, service accounts, and human users can only reach the data they are explicitly authorized to access, preventing accidental or unauthorized exposure of sensitive records.

Schema flexibility: The ability to add or modify the structure of stored data without requiring system downtime or complex migrations. As AI models and retrieval strategies evolve, this allows teams to update their data structures without disrupting production operations.

Semantic similarity: A measure of how closely related two pieces of content are in meaning, regardless of whether they share the same words. Vector search uses this property to find relevant results: by comparing the position of two vectors in high-dimensional space, the system determines how conceptually close a query is to stored content.

Sharding: A method of distributing data across multiple servers, called shards, so that storage capacity and query throughput can scale horizontally. Each shard holds a portion of the total dataset, allowing a system to grow from thousands of records to tens of millions without requiring a rebuild of the underlying architecture.

System sprawl: The fragility and operational complexity that results from stitching together multiple disconnected, specialized tools to perform tasks a unified platform could handle. In AI systems, sprawl typically means separate stores for operational data, embeddings, and search, each requiring synchronization, adding latency, and creating additional points of failure.

Vector embeddings: Numerical representations of content, such as text, images, or structured records, expressed as lists of numbers. Each representation captures the semantic meaning of its source, enabling a search system to find related items by comparing positions in high-dimensional space rather than matching exact words.

Vector search: A search technique that finds results based on semantic similarity rather than keyword overlap. The system converts a query into a numerical representation and locates the stored content whose representation is closest to it, allowing AI applications to respond to how users naturally phrase questions, even when their language differs from the source material.

Other Books You May Enjoy

If you enjoyed this book, you may be interested in these other books by Packt:

Architectures for the Intelligent AI-Ready Enterprise

Boris Bialek, Sebastian Rojas Arbulu, Taylor Hedgecock

ISBN: 978-1-80611-715-4

- Design AI-ready data architectures that scale in production
- Define systems of action and explain why they matter for enterprises
- Modernize legacy systems for AI-ready, unified architectures
- Implement governance, privacy, and compliance frameworks for AI
- Explore real-world AI implementations for over six industries
- Deploy production RAG and agentic systems with MongoDB
- Apply semantic data protection in regulated industries
- Build domain-specific AI agents and intelligent copilots
- Apply MCP, causal AI, and multi-agent systems for future-ready architectures

High Performance with MongoDB

Asya Kamsky, Ger Hartnett, Alex Bevilacqua

ISBN: 978-1-83702-262-5

- Diagnose and resolve common performance bottlenecks in deployments
- Design schemas and indexes that maximize throughput and efficiency
- Tune the WiredTiger storage engine and manage system resources for peak performance
- Leverage sharding and replication to scale and ensure uptime
- Monitor, debug, and maintain deployments proactively to prevent issues
- Improve application responsiveness through client driver configuration

Packt is searching for authors like you

If you're interested in becoming an author for Packt, please visit authors.packt.com and apply today. We have worked with thousands of developers and tech professionals, just like you, to help them share their insight with the global tech community. You can make a general application, apply for a specific hot topic that we are recruiting an author for, or submit your own idea.

Share your thoughts

Now you've finished *Future-Ready Data Foundation with MongoDB*, we'd love to hear your thoughts! Scan the QR code below to go straight to the Amazon review page for this book and share your feedback or leave a review on the site that you purchased it from.

https://packt.link/r/1807607178

Your review is important to us and the tech community and will help us make sure we're delivering excellent quality content.

www.ingramcontent.com/pod-product-compliance
Lightning Source LLC
LaVergne TN
LVHW022306200926
848481LV00004B/1236

9781807607173